THE SECRET POWER OF PYRAMIDS

Read this book and you will join us in our
immense admiration for the technological
geniuses of the past. Perhaps you, too, will
allow your imagination to take flight as you
muse with fond hope that the ancients
preserved for us the secret of universal
energy.

—The Authors.

To Noon + Either

The Secret Power of Pyramids

Bill Schul and
Ed Pettit

*I hope, you'll enjoy to read
this book, to discover how
to use the power in pyre-
mids to better your life!*

*Sincerely Yours,
Florence Vukotic*

CORONET BOOKS
Hodder Fawcett, London

Dedicated to INEZ and JEANN'E
Copyright © 1975 by Fawcett Publications, Inc.

First published 1975 by Fawcett
Publications, Inc., New York

Coronet Edition 1976
Third Impression 1978

Printed in Great Britain for
Hodder Fawcett Ltd., Mill Road, Dunton Green,
Sevenoaks, Kent (Editorial Office: 47 Bedford Square,
London WC1 3DP) by
C. Nicholls & Company Ltd,
The Philips Park Press, Manchester

ISBN 0 340 21012 5

Contents

Dedicated to INEZ and JEANN'E

Acknowledgments

The authors wish to express their appreciation to all who have helped in the compilation of this book.

They are especially grateful to Borderland Sciences Research Foundation which provided research information and sources and was kind enough to make drawings and photographs available. Our special thanks to Fred Schul and Rebecca Mayo for their excellent sketches, and to Carl D. Knepper for his consultation on electrical field theory.

We are grateful to the many individuals throughout the country who passed along information, experiences, and descriptions of their results with pyramid research and allied fields.

Lastly the authors are grateful to their respective helpmates, without whose encouragement and support the book would never have been written.

PREFACE

No other man-made object has claimed man's attention and wonderment as the Great Pyramid at Gizeh. The largest, heaviest, oldest, and most perfect structure created by human hands continues to overwhelm the imagination, to defy explanation, and to mystify its examiners. So ancient that its origin becomes lost in the shadows of time, it continues to offer up ever new knowledge of man and his environment. Curiously enough, as man's body of scientific knowledge grows, the Great Pyramid, like an embodied and immortal oracle, appears to anticipate the answers. Perhaps it is this encoded and seemingly unending storehouse of wisdom, ever unfolding to those wise enough to unlock its mysteries, that retains through the centuries for the Great Pyramid a central position in man's search for the hows and whys of his existence. And perhaps it is not too poetic to imagine that hidden somewhere in its history, its mathematical perfection, its purpose for being, are man's long-sought answers to his own destiny. Surely, then, the Great Pyramid would be the Philosopher's Stone.

But while the Great Pyramid was confounding experimentation and tantalizing its investigators to construct better technologies, it charitably offered up one of its many secrets—its shape alone conjured up known and unknown forms of energy affecting both animate and inanimate objects. No sooner had the discovery been made by the Frenchman M. Bovis, that structures built to the exact ratio of the Great Pyramid and placed in the same manner on the north-south magnetic axis would mummify meat, preserve food, sharpen razor blades, etc., than a whole new set of questions was launched concerning the nature of unexplained energy fields—to say nothing of the fresh wonderment about the pyramid itself.

Bovis's discovery and the followup work by a Czechoslovakian radio engineer, Karel Drbal, were reported in *Psychic Discoveries Behind the Iron Curtain,* by Ostrander and Schroeder. The book, which has claimed a tremendous following in this country and abroad, set loose a stampede of basement tinkerers and tool-shed experimenters, along with professional researchers. Discussion groups and experimental research clubs sprang up around the country to share findings and ideas on the subject. Several newsletters were established and widely circulated.

In the three years since the adventure was launched some very interesting and thought-provoking results have emerged. The effects on persons sitting, sleeping, meditating in pyramid structures have some implication to the fields of physiology, psychology, and metaphysics. Shortened healing time, relief from headaches, better relaxation, weight loss for overweight people, rejuvenation, etc., should say something to the medical profession. Results from meditating within the pyramid and heightened psychic sensitivity should interest the metaphysician and those interested in transcendental states. The effects on plant growth and seed germination should arouse the interest of the horticulturist. And food and water purification and preservation should claim the attention of every concerned person.

The new adventures with pyramids offer exciting possibilities to persons from all walks of life—the research scientist and the home-workshop buff, the philosophical discourser and the physics student looking for a project. The results of this involvement, however, may have some significance in our constant search for a greater understanding of ourselves and our environment.

Primarily, this book has been written with the hobbyist, lay scientist, and the curious in mind. Some background on the Great Pyramid itself is offered the reader in order that his own experiments with pyramidal shapes can envelop a wider perspective. Various experiments with pyramids are reported on as are our extensive investigations in the field. Included are plans for building pyramids.

If you are successful in your experiments, we feel you will join us in our immense admiration for the technological geniuses of the past. Perhaps you, too, will allow your imagination to take flight as you muse with fond hope that the ancients preserved for us the secret of universal energy.

1. THE PYRAMID:
ANCIENT & NEW MIRACLE WORKER

It is a point of sustained delight to the mystic, of reoccurring wonderment to the philosopher, and unceasing embarrassment to the scientist that the oldest man-made structure on the face of the earth continues to elude comprehension by the most brilliant of analytic minds.

We can probe the nature of protoplasm, extract workable concepts of the DNA and RNA life structures, utilize the coherent light of the laser beam, divide the atom, float laboratories in space, and yet the most ancient technological offerings of our forebears defy our examination.

We would like to have our predecessors' belief that we constantly contribute to our body of knowledge, generation after generation progressing to higher and more sophisticated understanding of our environment and ourselves.

We would like to imagine that despite our political and religious fervor and our superstitions, which drove us to burn libraries, demolish shrines, or turn away from knowledge, nothing of value was really lost or, if so, only temporarily, and that contemporary man has pushed beyond any ancient horizons of truth. We even get away with such claims for a time—until someone asks why it is that information now coming to light about the ancients' understanding of consciousness, of the human nervous and bioelectrical systems, continues to anticipate anything we have thus far learned by way of physiology and psychology; why it is we are unable to cut, drill, or match stone as ably as our forebears, who could fit limestone and granite boulders of the Great Pyramid together with a precision only today matched by opticians who perform their work on very small units; why it is, with all of our heavy construction equipment, we cannot move those large stones—some weighing seventy tons—into place without ramps; why it is that our mathematics continues to struggle for an equality with that of the ancients in the measurement of the earth and the movement of planetary bodies.

Where does this leave us in our belief in human progress? No one can ignore the monumental steps mankind has taken. We have too much evidence of progress in at least physical science to imagine that advancement is only an illusion. Why is it then that we find ourselves at times stumbling over some prehistoric artifacts that clearly point to a level of human accomplishment that we can only hope to emulate? When did such plateaus of sophistication exist? Where did it come from and why was it lost? Today, we can technologically achieve almost anything more efficiently than our ancestors could—anything, that is, that we know of. The Great Pyramid is one of those exceptions. The evidence to date, then, would seem to indicate that the notable exceptions point to a highly advanced civilization preceding us upon this globe some time back in the shadows of prehistory, and that this knowledge was somehow lost.

There is at least one other possible explanation. We

can ask along with von Däniken and other questioning writers if somewhere along the way there wasn't some input from higher intelligences from some other place in space. Such queries prompt us to look again within sacred texts and mythologies for references to earthly visitations from gods out of the heavens. And each time we pick up a newspaper and notice an item on alleged U.F.O. sightings, we cannot help but ponder.

There is a third possibility: The input of higher intelligence comes from a superior mind source, with the ideas or concepts materializing in certain men's minds in the form of intuitive knowledge, i.e., revelation. Both religion and metaphysics have long claimed the reality of this form of knowledge. Such knowing is allegedly not dependent upon man's ability to reason, but instead comes to him more or less complete.

According to Dr. Robert Assagioli, the founder of psychosynthesis, ". . . intuitive awareness comes to replace intellectual, logical and rational consciousness, or better, to integrate and transcend it. The intuition in fact leads to identification with what is seen and contemplated, and to the recognition of the intrinsic unity between object and subject."

In Paul Brunton's *Wisdom of the Overself* we find the following:

"What we have now to grasp is that there exists a part of the mind which seems unconscious to us but which really has an extraordinary and marvelous consciousness of its own. There is indeed a secondary consciousness which underlies our ordinary and familiar consciousness. A sound metaphysic therefore cannot limit the use of the term 'mind' only to its particular thinking phase of 'consciousness' alone. Mind is more than consciousness as we know it. . . ."

That concepts can enter the human mind that appear to originate elsewhere is told by the great 19th-century chemist Kekulé when he relates how a series of deep reveries led to his theory of molecular constitution. The information that came to him in his dream state has been called "the most brilliant piece of prediction to be found in the whole range of organic chemistry."

Einstein contended that his ideas on relativity were not "thought out" but came to him. Robert Louis Stevenson's ability to dream publishable plots by commanding "the brownies" of his mind to furnish him with a story is well known. Well known, too, is Poincaré's description of mathematical ideas rising in clouds, dancing before him, and colliding and combining into the first Fuschian Function as he lay in bed awaiting sleep.

Yet, whatever the source of information, the construction of the Great Pyramid demanded an ingenuity unsurpassed in the known history of the world.

Perhaps it has been the romanticist in man that attracts him to the mysteries of the unknown, or perhaps the bearing of some godlike seed deep within his breast that will not allow him rest until all the answers are contained within. The Pyramid is there, substantially there, known to his grandfather's grandfather as far back as man can remember, and its existence haunts his compulsion to know all that remains in his path. Even from the moon and the ocean floor man glances now and then to the stone enigma still awaiting his scientific or spiritual maturity, and man still wonders which. And standing equally silent by is the Pyramid's companion, the Sphinx, stoic beholder of civilization's passing parades and eternal sentry of the secrets of the Gizeh plain. For whom do they wait? What key must we find within our universe or within ourselves?

But now that the Great Pyramid can no longer be dismissed as a man-made mountain of stone designed to serve an inconsequential role as a tomb, perhaps man will eventually knock successfully at its portals by taking every possible purpose it might serve seriously until proven otherwise. At least such an approach will call for the best that is within us. If the fruits then prove to be unworthy, we can pass on by with no need for more backward glances.

One piece of recent evidence surrendered by the Great Pyramid would appear to have—as one might expect—universal application. The pyramidal shape, with the precise ratios of the Great Pyramid and centered on the true north-south axis, seems to reflect, generate, accumulate, or in some manner make available certain energy fields.

Pyramid models varying in size from a few inches to a number of feet have been constructed and used to house a variety of both animate and inanimate objects, including human beings. At this writing, the research would seem to indicate that the material out of which the models are constructed has little bearing on the results. Small pyramids have usually been made from cardboard and wood, and the larger pyramids have been made of wood, fiberglass, glass, and plastic sheeting. The presence of metal in or on the pyramid would seem to both inhibit and enhance the electromagnetic properties of the energy spectrum, depending upon the placement and relative amount of the metal. That the material used in the construction of the pyramid has proven significance remains the task of additional research. What results have been determined and some of the theories concerning the use of various materials will be discussed in later chapters.

The length of time that objects are left in the pyramid has been directed by the results obtained on a trial-and-error basis. For example, food commodities have been left in pyramids for several weeks and individuals have remained inside larger pyramids from a few minutes to a number of hours. The results reported include preservation of food items, purification of water, increased growth of plants, shortened germination period for seeds, removal of tarnish from metals, and for human subjects greater relaxation, improved contemplative and meditative states, healing, tranquility, and even rejuvenation.

The excitement over homemade pyramids was launched with the publication of *Psychic Discoveries Behind the Iron Curtain*, by Sheila Ostrander and Lynn Schroeder, in 1970. In the section on Czechoslovakian research, the authors tell of coming across various small pyramids being used as razor blade sharpeners. Through their inquiries they learned that several years ago a Frenchman, Monsieur Bovis, discovered that dead animals found in the King's Chamber of the Great Pyramid had not decayed but instead had dehydrated and mummified. It struck him that the shape of the Pyramid might have a significance. He built a pyramid about two-and-a-half feet tall and placed a dead cat directly under the apex and about one-third the distance from the base to the apex, where the King's Chamber is located. The cat mummified.

Bovis's published reports of his research with organic matter attracted the attention of Czechoslovakian radio and television engineer Karel Drbal. After experiments with several small models of the Cheops Pyramid, Drbal told Ostrander and Schroeder, "There's a relation between the shape of the space inside the pyramid and the physical, chemical, and biological process going on inside that space. By using suitable forms and shapes, we should be able to make processes occur faster or delay them."

Turning his attention to metal, Drbal wondered if the edge of a razor blade—which has a crystal structure and becomes dull after use—couldn't be returned to its original shape if placed within the heightened energy field of the pyramid. It worked to the tune of 50 to 200 shaves from a single blade. That was in the 1950s and cardboard- and styrofoam-pyramid razor blade sharpeners are now a common thing in Czechoslovakia and parts of Russia, and it is not too uncommon today to run into someone in this country with a homemade sharpener. We've yet to discover anyone who claims the pyramid models won't work if made to the right dimensions and placed directly on the south-north axis. Our experiments also bear out, as Ostrander and Schroeder claimed, that blue blades work better than stainless-steel ones.

Since the publication of *Psychic Discoveries Behind the Iron Curtain,* a number of experiments have been made by an assortment of investigators, including our own research with three-dozen models of a wide range of sizes, materials, and research objects. Although these explorations will be discussed in later chapters, along with plans for building pyramids and some suggestions for experimentation, it might be worthwhile to outline some of the investigations in order to give you an overview of the exciting possibilities.

—Tarnished jewelry and coins apparently are polished by energy forces working within the pyramid.

—Polluted water has been purified by being placed within a pyramid for several days, according to laboratory reports, and one wonders if blessed or holy water is not a physical reality.

—Milk remains fresh for several days and eventually turns into yogurt whereas milk in an identical container immediately outside the pyramid sours. A French firm has patented a pyramidal-shaped container for making yogurt, and an Italian milk company uses pyramidal-shaped cartons for its milk.

—Mummifies and dehydrates meat, eggs, etc.

—Flowers dehydrate but retain their form and color.

—Cuts, bruises, burns, etc, apparently heal faster after being exposed to the space within the pyramid. Toothaches and migraine headaches have reportedly been eliminated, and several persons have claimed relief from rheumatism and arthritis after sitting for a time in a pyramid. It is, of course, much too early in the experimental stages to make any claims. Again, we are touching base on possibilities initiated by reports from a variety of sources and the results received from our own experiments.

—Plants grow more rapidly inside than outside the pyramids.

—After using water treated in a pyramid as a face lotion for five weeks, Mrs. Pettit found her friends asking about her youthful appearance.

—Treated water seems to serve as a digestive aid, and when used on a wound, apparently makes it heal faster.

—Aluminum foil, treated for a time in a pyramid prior to using as a wrap for baking meat, greatly reduced the cooking time. The treated foil made into the shape of a hat and worn on top of the head seems to get rid of headaches and fosters relaxation.

—The taste of coffee, wine, fruit juice, etc., is improved when placed in a pyramid for a time, according to a number of separate test subjects.

—Food stuffs placed in a garbage container in the shape of a pyramid dehydrate without creating an odor.

—Persons who have sat in pyramids for several minutes to several hours have reported feeling more relaxed and vitalized. A number have claimed that meditation is much easier within the pyramid. After one young teenage girl started sleeping inside a pyramid her mother reported that the child was less nervous and had lost some unneeded weight.

How many of these experiments will stand the rigors of further exploration and rigid scientific testing only time will tell. Yet, sufficient work has been accomplished to date that one can safely venture that something is going on of a nonordinary nature within the pyramid space. It seems equally justified to say that energy fields, both known and unknown, are at play and that a greater understanding of these forces may well have tremendous implications for not only the scientific researcher but for each and every one of us. As modern physics has shown, *we* are energy and live in an energy universe, all interacting, and we talk less today about mind and matter and more about levels, degrees, and types of energy fields. It would follow, then, that a greater understanding of the nature of energy or energies would be an important key to the greater knowledge of ourselves—physically, mentally, and spiritually—and the world in which we live. If the pyramid shape does in some manner generate or accumulate usable energy, it can be an exciting adventure for all of us in seeking to unravel the mystery.

We understand how gravity and magnetism work while yet failing to understand what it really is and why it works. And likely we will discover how some of the energy fields work within the pyramid long before we truly understand their nature. We are just beginning to understand some of the rules of psychic phenomena, such as telepathy, psychometry, dowsing, and psychokinesis. Thanks to the ingenuity of recent technology, instruments are allowing us to objectively explore the psychic talents of gifted persons. Research to date would indicate this phenomena occurs through the medium of energy frequencies some of which are of such a subtle nature that they were experienced consciously only by psychic sensitives until the development of instruments responsive to these forces.

What we need to bear in mind, then, in our investigations is that the pyramid is not isolated; it exists within an environment permeated by energy fields. The task would seem to be one of determining how these energy fields function differently within the pyramid from outside it. One working hypothesis would be that all containers of space from the largest to the smallest affect energy fields in some manner, whether to enhance, modify, or inhibit them.

In a book, *Waves From Forms,* written a number of years ago by L. Turenne, a French engineer and professor of radio, it was explained that various forms, such as cones, pyramids, spheres, and cubes, act as different types of resonators for the energy in the universe—cosmic rays, solar rays, etc. The question asked by Turenne and by many others is what effect do these various forms have on human beings? We spend a large portion of our lives in various containers: rooms of different shapes, cars, trains, planes, and amphitheaters.

Ostrander and Schroeder quoted Drbal as saying that some of the forms are healthy for human beings, that the sphere and pyramid are two such forms. He contended that researchers are of the opinion that if hospitals were built in sphere or pyramid form patients would get well quicker. It is a curious thing that some people are bothered with claustrophobia in certain rooms or close quarters while others are not.

Buckminster Fuller has long contended that we should pay much greater attention to the forms of our buildings. His geodesic bubble would apparently be a healthy environment. Architects in Saskatchewan, Canada, have constructed trapezoidal rooms and irregular corridors in a mental hospital and discovered that the new environment was beneficial to patients.

So, unusual energy fields are not the private property of pyramids, but so far the pyramid has yielded the most exciting possibilities.

Of all the shapes and forms to be found in the universe the human being is the most diverse and complex user, modifier, and creator of energy forces. He is a universe within himself. And since he is always vitally involved in the experiments—planning, designing, building, handling materials, examining, analyzing—he cannot be totally divorced from the results. The question always remains as to what effect the experimenter has on the experiment.

We have become well aware of the human being's ability to manipulate physical matter without the use of physical force. Demonstrations of psychokinesis (ability to move or alter objects by psychic means) by such individuals as Nelya Kulagina, Alla Vinogravada, H. H. Rama, Uri Geller, and others have been successfully carried out under the strictest of laboratory conditions. The phenomena of mentally projecting images onto film by Ted Serios is another example, as is the ability of healer Dr. Olga Worrall to alter the electrical emission from plants as shown by high-frequency photography. Other healers have mummified meat and altered the chemical properties of water by holding the objects in their hands. Cleve Backster has registered the electrical patterns in plants by means of thought messages, and Marcel Vogel has changed the structure of microscopic life forms by means of thought images. There are innumerable instances of poltergeists moving physical objects by means of unconscious psychic emanations of which they were not always aware. The absence of the experimenter from the experiment does not of itself eliminate him as an influencing factor. Backster was able to affect the response of his plants from hundreds of miles away; Dr. Robert Miller registered profound changes in test plants during demonstrations of the influence of prayer on plants although those praying were nearly a thousand miles distant. Douglas Dean, by means of a plethysmograph, has demonstrated that the blood volume of a subject changes upon the moment of receiving a telepathic message. Geller bent spoons and forks over television waves.

Psychosomatic medicine has shown that our thoughts, attitudes, and even unconscious motivations have effects on our physical bodies. Anyone who has experienced a headache during tension or become nauseated from stage fright can confirm the reality of mind over matter. That thoughts and feelings, although unexpressed, can influence others has been measured by monitoring energy levels of subjects. Dr. John Pierrakos, a psychiatrist, noticed that the plants in his office wilted in the presence of depressed patients.

Blind studies, where the test subject is unaware of which object has been treated until after his reactions have been recorded, help reduce the degree of influence exerted by the human component. And double blind studies, where neither the subject nor the experimenter know which object is which until after the results are recorded, are even less corruptible. For example, if the research is the testing of the sharpness of razor blades, blind study would have the subject try both the treated and the control blades without knowing which was which. A double blind study would involve marking the two blades in a fashion that neither the subject nor the experimenter would know one set from the other until after the results were recorded. This approach would, say, keep the experimenter from sending a telepathic message to the subject, even though he might not do it consciously. We used time-lapse photography to measure the growth and movement of plants inside and outside the pyramids and were not present during the recording. Nevertheless, that does not completely eliminate our unconsciously influencing the plants from a distance.

The fact that we may minimize but are unable to reduce the influence of the human factor to zero in our experiments should not discourage our efforts. This is the case with all types of research, a fact that scientists are coming more and more to accept. Former astronaut Edgar Mitchell retired from the space program to devote his time and energy to parapsychological studies because he believed it carried a higher priority for the benefit of mankind. Speaking in 1972 at the annual convention of the American Psychiatric Association in Dallas, Captain Mitchell stated that science had reached that point in its growth where the experimenter could no longer eliminate himself from his experiments. He did not view this personal involvement as a detriment to research; rather he saw this occurrence as a higher level of scientific endeavor through which new knowledge of the vast dimensions of man would unfold. This greater knowledge of man himself would, then, open new doors for the understanding of the universe, Mitchell believed. Mitchell, who has a doctorate degree in science, recently founded the Institute of Noetic Sciences (noetics—the study of consciousness).

This spirit of personal involvement and unfoldment would seem to be the right one for us as we work with pyramids, for the more we learn about the purpose of the Great Pyramid the stronger become our suspicions that it was built as an instrument for human growth. It has become more and more apparent that we can uncover the secrets of the Great Pyramid only at the rate that we learn about our own dimensions. This would seem to have been the intention of the great builders.

2. THE HISTORICAL ENIGMA

The oldest and largest standing construction of man. To ponder that fact is to launch even the mildly curious in search of answers to many whats, whys, and whens. The history of pyramids and particularly the Great Pyramid is a fascinating study; the legends are even more intriguing. In the course of a single chapter, however, we can hardly offer more than an outline of some of the more significant facts and events. Hopefully a kind of overview will serve our turn in drawing the highlights into sufficient focus to serve as backdrops for current explorations.

The mystique that surrounds the Great Pyramid is not diminished with familiarity. On the contrary, the more one learns of its history, construction, and purpose the more the mystery becomes compounded. Endeavors to cover the subject adequately have been the design of many books, and a number of these are listed in the bibliography for those interested in additional reading. We would not intrude on their tasks here, for such ambition might be likened to trying to engrave a dictionary on the head of a pin. Rather, our job will be to touch base here and there with the past in order to set the stage for present considerations.

Some may ask why attention is directed primarily to the Great Pyramid of Gizeh when there are many other pyramids. True, pyramids were discovered in many parts of the world, including South America, China, the Himalayan mountains, Siberia, Mexico, Central America, Cambodia, France, England, and the United States, along with the 30 major and many minor pyramids in Egypt. Why, then, all the interest in the Great Pyramid, or Cheops Pyramid, as it is sometimes called? Primarily because it is the largest, the most perfect mathematically and geometrically, and because of certain features missing in other pyramids.

It is believed the Great Pyramid represents the epitome of Egyptian knowledge and that if secrets are to be uncovered it will happen within or around its portal. Traditional scholarship places the Great Pyramid somewhere in the early period of pyramid building, in the Fourth Dynasty. Six major pyramids allegedly preceded it and 23 followed it, according to Egyptian scholar I. E. S. Edwards, author of *The Pyramids of Egypt*. Some students believe the pyramids built prior to the Great Pyramid are indicative of a less sophisticated period and those following represent either a deterioration or corruption of knowledge and craftsmanship.

The Great Pyramid stands ten miles west of Cairo on the man-leveled one-mile-square plateau of the Gizeh Plain, overlooking from a height of 130 feet the palm groves of the Nile valley. The Great Pyramid's base covers slightly more than 13 acres and it is leveled to a fraction of an inch. More than 2,600,000 blocks of granite and limestone—weighing from two to 70 tons each—rise to its present height of over 450 feet. The perfectly hewn blocks to within one-one hundredth of an inch are so accurately put together that the joints are never more than one-fiftieth of an inch wide. It has been estimated that the Pyramid contains more solid masonry than all the cathedrals, churches, and chapels built in England since the time of Christ.

Standing with the Great Pyramid are two other pyramids, one slightly smaller and attributed to Cheops's successor, Kephren, and another pyramid, smaller still, attributed to Kephren's successor, Mykerinos. These, along with six smaller pyramids, allegedly built for Cheops's wives and daughters, form what is known as the Gizeh complex.

Originally, the Great Pyramid was covered with a mantle or veneer of polished limestone, making the sides smooth rather than stepped. Some time after the early part of the thirteenth century A.D. a series of earthquakes demolished large parts of northern Egypt. In the course of several generations the entire 22 acres of 100-inch thick covering of the pyramid was stripped to rebuild Cairo.

The Pyramid remained sealed for centuries; alas, any knowledge of an entrance was lost in remote antiquity. Then in 820 A.D. the young caliph, Abdullah Al-Mamum, son of Harun Al-Rashid, whose feats were to be celebrated in the *Arabian Nights,* heard of great treasures and priceless documents stored within the Pyramid. Along with a host of engineers, architects, builders, and stone masons, Al-Mamum searched for days along the smooth stone surface for an entrance. Failing to find one, the caliph decided to bore straight into the solid rock of the structure. But hammers and chisels could not scratch the stone. Refusing to give up the venture, Al Mamum resorted to heating the stone until it was red hot and then poured cold vinegar on it to crack the boulders. Battering rams were then used to chip away at the stone. After burrowing a small tunnel for 100 feet, Al-Mamum was prepared to abandon the project when a workman heard what appeared to be a large stone sliding into place somewhere not far from where they were working. They renewed their efforts, tunneled toward the sound and broke into a passage little more than three feet high and three feet wide.

The passageway sloped at a steep angle, but the Arabs struggled up the tunnel and discovered the original secret entrance, which had been placed 49 feet above the base of the Pyramid. Al-Mamum and his men made their way down the low, treacherous Descending Passage cut deep into the rock of the plateau, but at the bottom of what has become known as "the Pit" they found nothing but dust and debris. On the far side of the Pit they found an even narrower horizontal tunnel that led 50 feet to a blank wall. In the floor was what appeared to be a well shaft. It was carved to a depth of 30 feet and led nowhere.

Retracing their steps to the large stone that had fallen in the Descending Passage, Al-Mamum and his men speculated that the stone had covered a large red granite plug, which blocked another passage sloping up into the body of the Pyramid. The granite plug proved impregnable, so they cut around it through the softer limestone. Two more granite plugs blocked the passage and after the granite many limestone blocks followed. Still the workers persisted and finally emerged into an ascending passage with a low ceiling. Crawling on their knees, the men made their way up 150 feet of slippery rock, then into another tunnel with an equally low ceiling. At the end of the second tunnel they found themselves in a bare room approximately 18 feet square and with a gabled ceiling. As the Arabs placed their women in tombs with gabled ceilings, the room became known as the "Queen's Chamber." But nothing was to be found here but an empty niche in the east wall.

The Arabs retraced their steps to the Ascending Passage, and, raising their torches, they discovered a void above them. By climbing on each others' shoulders they could reach high enough to see that they were at the bottom of a narrow but high gallery. It stretched upward at the same slope as the Ascending Passage for approximately 157 feet and was 28 feet high. At the end of their climb they came upon a huge stone about three feet high, which proved to be a six-by-eight-foot platform. Beyond the platform the floor was level but the ceiling was only three and a half feet high. This formed a sort of entrance to a small antechamber. Another short and low passage followed and Al-Mamum and his men found themselves in a large room, the walls, floor, and ceiling of polished red granite. This room, 34 feet long, 17 feet wide, and nineteen feet high, became known as the King's Chamber.

Frantically the Arabs searched for treasures, but all that was to be found was an empty sarcophagus made of highly polished, dark chocolate-colored granite.

Al-Mamum paid off his men—and possibly saved his own throat—by planting gold in one of the chambers and seeing to it that they dug it up, or so the legend goes. In any case so ended the first attempt to make the great structure give up its secrets.

Along came the earthquakes of 450 years later; the stone casing was stripped from the outside, but no one was to enter the Pyramid again for several centuries. Superstition surrounded the Pyramid. It allegedly was inhabited by ominous spirits and was filled with vermin and serpents. A twelfth-century adventurer, Rabbi Benjamin ben Jonah of Navarre, claimed that the Pyramid was constructed by witchcraft. Abd-al-Latif, a teacher of medicine and history in Baghdad, worked up his courage to step inside the Pyramid shortly after Benjamin's visit but is said to have fainted from fear and later claimed that he came out more dead than alive.

It was not until 1638 that the Great Pyramid was to gain another visitor. John Greaves, an English math teacher and astronomer, entered the Pyramid with hopes of finding treasure of a sort different from Al-Mamum's.

He sought the data that would establish the dimensions of the planet. After some effort Greaves made his way to the King's Chamber where, according to Peter Tompkins in his book *Secrets of the Great Pyramid,* he "was puzzled that so incredibly imposing a structure as the Pyramid should be built around a single chamber with a single empty coffer. He could see no apparent reason for its portcullis entrance or for the complexity of its ante-chamber where the walls changed mysteriously from limestone to granite. But being a scientist by nature, Greaves set to collecting and noting data about the building."

Greaves discovered another mysterious part of the Pyramid—a section that also served no apparent purpose. Along the ramp of the Grand Gallery Greaves uncovered a stone block that led to a passage straight down into the bowels of the Pyramid. The tunnel was slightly over three feet wide. However, notches had been dug along the side, and Greaves lowered himself 60 feet into the "well" where the shaft was enlarged into a small chamber or "Grotto," as it is now called. The shaft continued for a short way below the Grotto and ended. Greaves devoted the remainder of his stay to mathematics, measuring carefully everything within and without the Pyramid.

Greaves's measurements of the Pyramid gained the attention of Sir Isaac Newton, who subsequently wrote a paper entitled "A Dissertation upon the Sacred Cubit of the Jews and the Cubits of Several Nations: In which, from the dimensions of the Great Pyramid, as taken by Mr. John Greaves, the ancient Cubit of Memphis is determined."

"Newton's preoccupation with establishing the cubit of the ancient Egyptians was no idle curiosity," Tompkins states, "nor just a desire to find a universal standard of measure; his general theory of gravitation, which he had not yet announced, was dependent on an accurate knowledge of the circumference of the earth. All he had to go on were the old figures of Eratosthenes and his followers, and on their figures his theory did not work out accurately."

Greaves's measurements of the exterior of the Pyramid failed to be accurate because of the debris at the base, and Newton's theory of gravitation was to be based a few years later on the findings of the French astronomer Jean Picard. Little did Newton, his followers, and critics know that the Sphinx could be used as a geodetic marker to indicate the equinox, and that it once had between its paws an obelisk whose shadow was used to compute the correct circumference of the earth and the variance in the degree of latitude.

Nathaniel Davison, later to serve as British Consul General in Algeria, lowered himself into the well discovered by Greaves and below the Grotto to the end of the shaft where he found only debris. Tompkins writes: "To Davison it appeared strange that anyone should go to such an enormous amount of effort to dig a shaft almost 200 feet into the heart of the Pyramid and simply come to a dead end. But there was nothing more he could do. It was extremely close and filthy at the bottom of the 'Well,' and his candle soon burnt up what little air was available. Also, an immense number of huge bats made it difficult for Davison to keep his candle lighted; so he laboriously made his way back to the surface."

Davison did, however, discover other features of the Pyramid. He spotted a small rectangular hole at the top of the Grand Gallery. With some difficulty he managed to crawl through this small hole and found a chamber as large as the King's Chamber but with a ceiling too low to stand under. The floor of the chamber was found to be nine monolithic granite slabs estimated to weigh up to 70 tons each. The underside of the slabs served as the ceiling for the King's Chamber. Further, the ceiling of this room above the King's Chamber was constructed of similar slabs.

This chamber, as with all others, failed to yield any treasures, artifacts of any sort, and not even an inscription. It was to be known as Davison's Chamber and later to serve as Captain G. B. Caviglia's living quarters.

Napoleon came to conquer Egypt, and with him arrived an entourage of French mathematicians and scientists, including Edme'-Francois Jomard and Colonel Jean Marie Joseph Coutelle who were to make more accurate measurements of the Pyramid than any previously taken. What helped them in their efforts was the clearing away of the debris at the base. They located the esplanade on which the Great Pyramid had been built and the large sockets set into the base rock where the cornerstones had been laid.

Shortly after the beginning of the nineteenth century, Captain Caviglia, master of a Maltese vessel, whose exploits are described elsewhere in this book, cleared the well shaft of debris and discovered that it connected with the Descending Passage. Colonel Howard-Vyse joined Caviglia in exploration of the Pyramid in 1836, and he discovered three additional chambers above Davison's and of approximately the same size. The chambers were separated by granite slabs and the upper-most was gabled with huge blocks of limestone. Howard-Vyse theorized that the five superimposed chambers were designed to relieve the flat ceiling of the King's Chamber from the pressure of the 200 feet of solid masonry above it.

Howard-Vyse also discovered two air-vent holes running through 200 feet of rock to the King's Chamber. When these were cleared of debris, fresh air kept the room at an even temperature of 68 degrees throughout the year.

As it became more and more evident that the Great Pyramid harbored neither gold, jewels, nor artifacts, and appeared less and less to be a tomb, scholars with a variety of interests and backgrounds speculated on the origin and the purposes for which it was designed. While traditional Egyptologists down to this day continue to contend that it was built as a tomb for Cheops, the evidence—thanks to the scholarship of John Taylor, Sir John Herschel, Piazzi Smyth, William Petrie, David Davidson, Robert T. Ballard, Moses B. Cotsworth, Joseph Norman Lockyer, Richard A. Proctor, Livio Stecchini, and others—leans strongly toward a much greater purpose or purposes.

Today's accumulation of evidence would indicate that the Great Pyramid enshrines a lost science. Is this, the last remaining of the Seven Wonders of the World, the creation of unknown architects who possessed a more profound knowledge of the universe than anyone who has followed them? Until very recently there was little proof that the Egyptians of five thousand years ago were capable of the precise astronomical calculations and mathematical solutions required to locate, orient, and build the Pyramid.

"It was attributed to chance that the foundations were almost perfectly oriented to true north, that its structure incorporated a value for pi (the constant by which the diameter of a circle may be multiplied to give its true circumference) accurate to several decimals," Tompkins states in his introduction. He points out that its main chamber incorporated the famous Pythagorean theorem, which Plato in his "Timaeus" claimed as the building block of the universe. "Chance was said to be responsible for the fact that the Pyramid's angles and slopes display an advanced understanding of trigonometric values," Tompkins continued, "and that its shape quite precisely incorporates the fundamental proportions of the 'Golden Section.'"

Today's mathematicians claim that the first rough use of pi in Egypt was not until 1700 B.C., at least a thousand years after the building of the Great Pyramid. Pythagora's theorem was supposedly devised during the fifth century B.C., and trigonometry was attributed to Hipparchus in the second century B.C. This is what we read in our textbooks. But now the whole subject of who did what when is subject to review.

"Recent studies of ancient Egyptian hieroglyphs and the cuneiform mathematical tablets of the Babylonians and Sumarians have established," Tompkins points out, "that an advanced science did flourish in the Middle East at least three thousand years before Christ, and that Pythagoras, Eratosthenes, Hipparchus, and other Greeks reputed to have originated mathematics on this planet merely picked up fragments of an ancient science evolved by remote and unknown predecessors. . . . The Great Pyramid, like most of the great temples of antiquity, was designed on the basis of a hermetic geometry known only to a restricted group of initiates, mere traces of which percolated to the Classical and Alexandrian Greeks."

These and many other discoveries, with the list continuing to grow, are demanding a new assessment of the Great Pyramid, a closer look at its history; actually a whole new framework of reference points appears mandatory. We are now in the position of seriously wondering if the builders of the Great Pyramid accomplished and knew a great deal more than we credit them with. The implications of the existence of this body of knowledge is explosive and far reaching. That the Great Pyramid was constructed as a mountainous tomb in order to satisfy some pharaoh's ego trip is a concept no longer tenable.

One must remember that no mummies were ever found in the Great Pyramid. The contention by some Egyptologists that the sarcophagi and the passages were sealed in order to protect the mummies of the pharoahs from thieves and spoilers hardly seem defensible when the so-called burial chamber was opened for the first time since sealing and was found empty.

Some scholars believe the Great Pyramid was built as a place of initiation: not only as the site of initiation by the Mystery Schools but also as an instrument of initiation. In other words, within this concept, the energy fields generated or enhanced by the Pyramid contribute to an elevation of consciousness.

In *The Secret Teaching of All Ages,* Manly Palmer Hall sees the Great Pyramid as the visible covenant between Eternal Wisdom and the world. The angles represent Silence, Profundity, Intelligence, and Truth. The triangular sides are symbolic of the three-fold spiritual power. The south side of the Pyramid represents Cold; the north side represents Heat; the west side signifies Darkness; and the east side, Light.

Hall considers the Great Pyramid to be the "first temple of the Mysteries," a repository of secret truths. Men entered the portals of the Great Pyramid and came out the illumined of antiquity. The drama of "The Second Death" was believed to have been enacted within the King's Chamber where the candidate for initiation was symbolically crucified and placed in the sarcophagus. The initiate would then experience the transition from the physical world to the transcendental levels of nature.

At one point during the ritual the sarcophagus was supposedly struck, producing an unusual tone. In the chapter, "The Voice of the Pyramid," we discuss experiments with sound as to its effects on material objects, plant growth, its use in therapy, and its ancient and modern use as a tool for influencing states of consciousness.

With the completion of the secret rites, the initiate was allegedly reborn, had experienced the second birth, and become a dweller of two worlds. He was then illumined or enlightened and possessed the knowledge of the world.

According to Yoga philosophy, the human possesses three levels of perception or experience: the physical, the psychic, and the noetic or spiritual. As the evolutionary processes unfold in man, he responds to himself and the world through not only his physical senses but also through the psychic perceptors. This is made possible by energy activating the chakras or vortices of energy within the etheric or electric envelope of the body. The heightened activity of the chakras or centers allows the individual to respond to not only physical stimuli but also psychical phenomena. Growing awareness and a heightened level of functioning then eventually lead to the simultaneous activation of all the chakras, a coursing of energy through the body and carrying consciousness to its highest level or spiritual awakening. This state is viewed as enlightenment, brought about by the higher tuning of man's psychophysiological mechanisms and expanding use of energy resources. With the activation of all seven chakras, the subject radiates a greater amount of light or halo. Energy flows up through the centers from its seat at the base of the spine and awareness becomes focused in the higher centers by means of an interaction between the pituitary gland and the pineal body in the brain. The flow of pranic energy through the centers is viewed by Yoga philosophy as the arousal of the Serpent Power, the rising of the Kundalini, or the Baptism by Fire.

Spiritual awakening can be brought about by several methods, according to this system, although none act in isolation or entirely apart from the other methods: 1. through the natural unfoldment of higher and higher levels of functioning brought about through the evolutionary processes and which can be retarded or quickened by the acts of the individual; 2. through the special assistance of a guru or teacher who is himself in control of this energy and can thereby direct it in such a fashion that it works upon the subject; and 3. through the use of special exercises, disciplines, and techniques designed to activate the chakras and raise the Kundalini power.

We are entertaining the hypothesis that the Great Pyramid was designed to serve as a device for activating higher energy levels and elevate consciousness. Our experiences, and those of others, with psychic ability being increased as a result of time spent within pyramids, might point to this being one of the design plans of the builders of the Great Pyramid. This subject is given additional attention in the chapter on altered states of consciousness.

Although the Arabs had long contended that the Great Pyramid was constructed as an astronomical observatory, it was not until the turn of the century that a reasonable solution was put forth as to how the polished sides and interior passages were used for observations.

British astronomer Richard Anthony Proctor came upon an old Roman document suggesting that the Great Pyramid would have served well as an observatory when constructed to the level of the Grand Gallery. This would have provided a large square platform where the ancient astronomers could have recorded the movements of the stars. They would have needed a true meridian across the heavenly vault in order to detect the moment when the stars, sun, and moon transited this meridian.

Proctor reasoned that the builders first constructed a huge graduated slot aligned on the meridian. From various levels along this slot they could observe the movement of the stars and their several transits.

In his book, *The Great Pyramid, Observatory, Tomb, and Temple,* Proctor describes how the architects would have proceeded to build such an observatory. In order to obtain a true north-south axis for their terrestrial meridian, they would have used the tops of a couple of pillars to focus on whatever star was nearest to the celestial north pole and find the top and bottom of its circular path. A line through the two points—easily measured with a plumb line—would be true north.

Once the ancient architects transferred a true meridian from the sky to the ground, they could have consolidated the line by digging into a descending passage through the rock, using their chosen star to guide the tunnel downward at exactly the angles of its rays. This tunnel, Proctor reasoned, would have provided perfect stability to the directional line and the longer the passage, the truer its orientation.

Proctor's theory provides an explanation for the perfect straightness of the walls of the Descending Passage. With the length of the Descending Passage and its angle of descent measured, the architects could have used elementary trigonometry to locate a central point immediately above the end of the Descending Passage as a center for the building of the Pyramid. Having a central point and a true meridian, the builders could have laid the socket holes for a square base and begun laying the stone courses on a leveled platform. Proctor believed that the architects could have obtained true levels by using water troughs in conjunction with the light rays from the star.

The tunnel could have been continued up through the lower tiers of stone, in order to maintain a precise direction for the lower tiers, until the tunnel reached the exterior of the Pyramid. In order to continue the accurate laying of the remaining tiers, Proctor reasoned that the builders created an ascending passage at exactly the same reflecting angle (26 degrees and 17 minutes) as the Descending Passage. They filled the Descending Passage with water and thereby could reflect the polar star back up the Ascending Passage, keeping the passage truly aligned and the Pyramid level.

Proctor notes that in order for the Descending Passage to hold water, the masonry would have to be of hard rock and carefully joined. Interestingly enough, the stones at this particular point are much harder than the rest of the passage and more finely joined.

But then the Ascending Passage suddenly changes to an overlapping gallery 28 feet wide. It serves no apparent role as an orientation for the construction of the stone courses, but must have served some significant purpose, Proctor reasoned, so outstanding was the architectural design and so carefully had it been constructed.

Proctor decided that if an ancient astronomer wished for a large observation slot exactly bisected by a meridian through the north pole in order to observe the transit of

the heavenly bodies, he would have requested of an architect an extremely high slit with vertical walls—a gallery whose aperture, using the reflection of the polar star,
would be designed to be bisected by a true meridian.
Peering through such a slot, the observer could watch the
passage of the panoply of the zodiac and note the transit
of each star across a perfect meridian. This is exactly
what today's astronomer does when he sets his transit circle to the vertical meridians.

Proctor hypothesizes that someone in the Queen's
Chamber could keep time by an hourglass or water clock
in coordination with other observers in the Grand Gallery
and signal either the beginning or the end of the transit
across the Gallery's field of view. Looking down the Descending Passage into a reflecting water pool, the astronomer could have determined the precise moment of a
star's transit as that is the only instant its rays will be reflected. Tompkins reminds us that this is the very same
system used today at the U.S. Naval Observatory in
Washington, D.C., where the daily transit of stars is noted
to a split second by their reflection in a pool of mercury.

Tompkins quotes George Sarton, professor of the history of science at Harvard, as stating that the astronomical ability of the early Egyptians "is proved not only by
their calendars, tables of star culminations, and tables of
star risings, but also by some of their instruments such as
ingenious sundials or the combination of a plumb line
with a forked rod that enabled them to determine the azi-
muth of a star."

Shortly after the turn of the century a succession of
pyramidologists attempted to prove the Great Pyramid
contained a 6,000-year prophetic history of the world,
starting in 4000 B.C. and going to 2045 A.D. These
prophecies were compared to the Bible. They envisioned
an allegory in stone in which the Descending Passage
represented humanity on its way down toward ignorance

and evil. Where the Descending Passage and the Ascending Passage joined, the evil spirits continued on to the Pit, while the rest of humanity, saved by the Christian Dispensation, moved upward along the Ascending Passage toward the Light of the Grand Gallery. Having passed beyond the Great Step, humanity must continue bent in submission through the Antechamber of Chaos before it could emerge in the King's Chamber and the glory of the Second Coming.

According to Tompkins, the Prophetic chronology was supposedly marked out along the passages and chambers, with one year corresponding to one Pyramid inch, starting with the first created man and ending with the Day of Judgment.

In his book, *The Source of Measure,* J. Ralston Skinner contends that the Great Pyramid was a temple of initiation. He linked the Pyramid to the Jewish cabala, a system of allegorical symbolism that allegedly sets forth the secret teachings of the Bible and reveals the great cosmic principles of man's origin.

When one considers today's wide following of the medieval prophet Nostradamus and such modern prophets as Edgar Cayce and Jeane Dixon, it is not difficult for many individuals to consider that ancient prophets left a record in stone. However, with current research into the nature of prophecy and studies in altered states of consciousness, most of the interest is now focused on the Great Pyramid and particularly its small imitations as instruments for inducing states of awareness with prophetic insight.

It has never been determined who built the Great Pyramid and when. No record has ever been found as to its construction. Egyptologists are not in complete accord but generally agree that it was built during the Fourth Dynasty, 2720 to 2560 B.C. The time of construction is usually given between 30 and 56 years.

But there are many dissenters. One thing that confounds scholars is that the construction of the pyramids, particularly the Great Pyramid of Gizeh, demonstrates a fully developed grasp of mathematics, astronomy, geography, navigation, engineering, architecture, etc., at the time of construction without a demonstrable period for learning these sciences.

A number have proposed that the builders were from the advanced civilization of Atlantis who constructed the Pyramid as a means of preserving all the known sciences, as well as providing a temple of initiation and a device for generating powerful energy fields.

This version has gained support from the readings of Edgar Cayce. According to Cayce, a group of nine hundred people entered Egypt from an advanced civilization around 12,000 B.C. With them was a young priest, Ra-Ta, who was a channel for the Creative Forces. Why had they chosen Egypt? Reading 281-42 states: "This had been determined by that leader or teacher (not physical leader, but spiritual interpreter or guide) as the center of the universal activities of nature, as well as the spiritual forces, and where there might be the least disturbance by the convulsive movements which came about in the earth through the destruction of Lemuria, Atlantis, and—in later periods—the flood."

Paramount of Ra-Ta's endeavors was the construction of the Great Pyramid, which would be an archtype through the ages. As such it was designed to incorporate—within the structure of its passageways and chambers, and in its mathematical and geometric relationships—the knowledge gained by those peoples, as well as the prophecies of the centuries yet to pass. This monumental structure also served, according to Cayce reading 5748-5, as a temple of initiation "of that sometimes referred to as the White Brotherhood," and was built by means other than pure physical labor, for the Atlanteans assisted in the construction. How was the Great

Pyramid built? "By the use of those forces in nature as make for iron to swim, stone floats in the air in the same manner." (5748-6)

Some scholars such as Piazzi Smyth and Joseph A. Seiss believed that the building of the Great Pyramid was made possible by the revelations of God. Erich von Däniken, et al., propose that the Great Pyramid, along with a number of other ancient structures, were designed by intelligences from outer space who visited this planet many thousands of years ago. Recent Russian authors postulate that the builders came from Indonesia some ten to twelve thousand years ago after their advanced civilization was destroyed by a natural catastrophe. The Russians claim to have found several objects to support this theory, including astronomical maps, and crystal lenses of such a nature that they can only be ground by an electrical process. In *Meetings With Remarkable Men* George Ivanovich Gurdjieff relates that he once obtained a map of pre-sand Egypt complete with pyramids and Sphinx.

One of the oldest dates for the Great Pyramid has been given by an Arab writer, Abu Zeyd el Balkhy, who claims to quote an ancient inscription to the effect that the Pyramid was built at a time when the Lyre was in the Constellation of Cancer, which has been interpreted as meaning "twice 36 thousand years before the Hegira," or around 73,000 years ago. This vintage would seem to correspond to some carbon-14 readings on the structure that would date it around 71,000 B.C., except that there is some questioning now as to the reliability of carbon-14 in measuring age.

As to the actual construction of the pyramids, controversy reigns here also. It is believed that most of the limestone blocks for the construction of the Great Pyramid were brought from the Mokattam quarries a few miles across the Nile, although some blocks would seem to come from the Gizeh hills. The nearest source for the 70-ton granite blocks used in the King's Chamber is the

Aswan quarry located near Syene, which is 500 miles up the Nile.

Some scholars seem satisfied that the 2,600,000 stone blocks, weighing from two to 70 tons, were quarried and finely tooled with copper instruments, then dragged on sleds or over rollers to barges, unloaded and dragged again to the construction site, and hoisted in place by ropes, pullies, slides, and wooden cranes.

Other writers find it hard to believe that primitive tools could have accomplished the task when today's architects and engineers with all their technical resources could not duplicate the feat.

Toth and Nielsen stat in *Pyramid Power:* "The engineering feats performed by the Egyptians in transporting and unloading rivals those performed today with the use of the modern techniques and equipment of our experts. This became evident in the 1960's when the Aswan Dam was nearing completion. A united effort was made by some engineers, using sophisticated equipment from all over the world, to save as many temples, palaces and statues as possible before the Aswan damming would inundate those colossal masterpieces forever. But all the modern equipment and expertise of the highly trained and skilled engineers could not lift many of the single monoliths. The stones actually had to be broken into smaller pieces in order to make the relocation attempt a reality. Because the experts needed to cut up the blocks of stone, which the Egyptians obviously had been able to handle intact, a very small percentage of the actual targeted edifices could be saved from the inundating waters of the Aswan Dam."

Study the Great Pyramid from any approach, in any of its many aspects, and one seems to wind up with several questions for every apparent answer. Though many have crawled over and through it with measuring tape, slide rule, chemicals, and instruments of all descriptions, the Great Pyramid remains an enigma.

3. MYSTERIOUS ENERGY FIELDS

The word "pyramid" comes from the Greek "pyro," meaning fire, and "amid," which means being at the center. Fire was one of the four properties of the universe in ancient cosmology, the others being earth, water, and air. As it was used in the ancient teachings, fire was defined as the universal energy, the vitality permeating all of life.

In a pamphlet entitled *The Pyramid and Its Relationship to Biocosmic Energy,* G. Patrick Flanagan, Ph.D., stated, "The major secret of the Great Pyramid of Giza, the Seventh Wonder of the World, is so obvious that it is hidden with the word pyramid. We shall attempt to demonstrate that biocosmic energy is the fire in the middle which has eluded scientists for thousands of years."

Current research of the "new" form of energy may supply the long-awaited clues to a host of happenings, from mental telepathy to ESP to spiritual healing.

Study of the mysterious energy is underway in a

number of laboratories. It is believed that an understanding of the laws governing this force will provide practical explanations to various psychic phenomena that to date have eluded the "hard data" scientists.

Newton's Law of Gravitation and Einstein's Theory of Relativity provided the explanations for understanding universal application of certain physical forces. So, too, the unveiling of the special "X" force is expected to provide the common denominator behind such phenomena as psychokinesis (PK)—the effect of thought on material objects—and the sending of telepathic messages over distances such as astronaut Edgar Mitchell's efforts to communicate from the moon.

"As we continue to unravel the qualities of this energy field and are able to define its laws, it would seem reasonable to propose that various kinds of so-called psychic phenomena occur as a result of this force and are not isolated and unrelated occurrences," said Dr. Stanley Krippner, director of the Dream Laboratory at the Maimonides Medical Center in Brooklyn, New York.

Study of the energy field has been the focal point of Soviet scientist Dr. Genady Sergeyev's tests of Nelya Mikhailova, the Leningrad housewife who has created an international sensation with her ability to move anything from teacups to cigarettes with her mind. Using a force-field detector, Dr. Sergeyev recorded intense radiation of electrostatic and electromagnetic fields four yards from Mrs. Mikhailova during a performance in an insulated electroencephalographic chamber, according to reports received in this country. Similar equipment has been used to measure and confirm the powerful PK power of Uri Geller.

Drs. Abram Hoffer and Harold Kelm at the University of Saskatchewan in Canada have researched the measurement of human force fields at a distance by using a detector consisting of two capacitor plates, a pre-amplifier, and a line recorder similar to an electrocardiograph. The detector charts the body's invisible energy field or electrical aura at a distance.

"In the world systems of occult physics is a concept of energy (and a related field theory) remarkably similar to that of modern physics. Namely, there is one primary form of energy from which everything else is constructed," Dr. Elmer Green, director of the Psycho-physiological Laboratory at the Menninger Foundation in Topeka, Kansas, stated. He added, "In occult physics, however, it is postulated that the elaborated structure of the one basic energy includes not just physical substance, but emotional substance, mental substance, and other more rarefied materials, and that in the human being all these materials are brought together."

Manly Palmer Hall, president of the Philosophical Research Association, Los Angeles, California, commenting on this, said, "The early Greeks explained that this union of the substances—symbolized by earth, water, fire, and air—was what made man the microcosm. In him, they said, were found all the materials of the macrocosm, the universe."

Sri Aurobindo, the Indian philosopher and teacher, wrote, "One can think of the universe as all spirit, with matter being the densest form; or one can think of the universe as all substance, with spirit being its most rarefied form."

The idea of bioenergy is not a new one. The ancient Chinese said that man is linked to the cosmos through vital energy that fills the universe. In India they refer to this force as "prana," in which everything is enveloped. Mesmer called it animal magnetism. Reichenbach referred to it as odic force. Blondot called it N-rays. Soviet scientists have entitled it bioplasmic energy; and Czech scientists call it psychotronic energy. While different names are used, there appears to be general agreement as to the characteristics of this energy.

Czech scientists Zdenek Rejdak and Karel Drbal have

written: "Human beings and all living things are filled with a kind of energy that until recently hasn't been known to Western science. This bioenergy, which we call psychotronic energy, seems to be behind PK; it may be the basis of dowsing. It may prove to be involved in all psychic happenings."

The Czechs have demonstrated to scientists from this country psychotronic generators, sometimes referred to as Pavlita generators after their inventor, Robert Pavlita. Charged with energy directed from human psychic force, the generators—constructed of various shapes from a variety of materials—reportedly move physical objects of either metallic or nonmetallic nature. The research is backed by the Czech Academy of Science.

In working with this energy, the Soviet scientists claim their "new discovery" of bioplasmic energy can be seen by anyone in photographs and electron microscopes, thanks to Kirlian photography. Semyon Kirlian invented a new process of photography, comprising some fourteen patents, which uses high-frequency electrical fields involving a generator that generates 75,000 to 200,000 electrical oscillations per second.

The Kirlian photographic process has now been developed in this country by a number of scientists, including Dr. Thelma Moss of U.C.L.A. and Henry Monteith of the University of New Mexico. As the teslacoil equipment for producing the electrical aura is relatively inexpensive, many home experimenters—including ourselves—have constructed the units and are studying the results.

Olga Worral, the internationally recognized healer, recently showed us a number of high frequency photographs taken at U.C.L.A. showing the aura around a torn leaf before and after she treated the leaf with healing energy. The photographs revealed a considerable increase in the size and activity of the aura following her administration of energy.

The Kirlian photographic process allegedly takes photos of the bioplasmic or etheric energy field surrounding and penetrating the human body and other living things. This field is likened by the scientists to the concept of the human aura, a radiating luminous cloud surrounding the body. Art from Egypt, Greece, and India revealed holy figures in a luminous aura before the artists of the Christian era painted saints with halos.

In her book, *Awareness,* the late famous psychic Eileen Garrett, and former president of the Parapsychology Foundation of New York, stated "I've always seen every plant, animal and person encircled by a misty surround." She also has reported seeing spirals of this same energy leaving the bodies of the recently dead up to three days after death.

Elsewhere in *Awareness,* Mrs. Garrett stated: "Throughout my whole life I have been aware of the fact that everyone possesses a second body—a double. The double is a distinct fact in Eastern and Theosophical teaching and as such it is said to be an energy body, a magnetic area associated with the physical human corpus, an area in which the immaterial forces of the cosmos, the solar system, the planet, and one's more immediate environment are normally transformed in the life and belief of the individual." She adds, "The double is the medium of telepathic and clairvoyant projection."

Dr. Wilden Penfield of McGill University in Montreal, Canada, has done a number of operations in which large segments of patients' brains have been removed. Dr. Penfield stated that the mind carried on as before. He ventured, "Perhaps we will always be forced to visualize a spiritual element—a spiritual essence that is capable of controlling the mechanism."

Swami H. H. Rama, during his recent visit to the Menninger Foundation, said, "The energy body—sometimes referred to as the astral body—can be used by a trained yogi for traveling by the consciousness apart from the physical body. At death, the individual leaves his flesh body and continues his life in the energy body." In all of his mind-over-matter experiments, Swami Rama referred to his ability to control his body and mind and to exhibit psychic insights as being in tune with pranic energy.

The projection of the energy body is currently under study by Dr. Charles Tart at the University of California at Davis, and by Harold Sherman, director of the ESP Research Associates Foundation in Arkansas. This is also the subject of a book issued by Doubleday entitled *Journeys Out of the Body,* authored by Charlottesville, Virginia, businessman Robert A. Monroe. He tells of some nine hundred trips outside his physical body. When we visited with him at the Interdisciplinary Conference on the Voluntary Control of Internal States, held at Council Grove, Kansas, and sponsored by the Menninger Foundation, he told us that when he left his physical body he seemed to enter or become an energy body.

Projection of this "X" energy has been reported by Dr. Bernard Grad of McGill University. He had a psychic healer hold a flask of water and then pour it on barley seed. The seed significantly outgrew the untreated seed, according to Dr. Grad. He further stated that this previously unacknowledged energy has the widest implications for medical science, from healing to lab tests.

In their book *Psychic Discoveries Behind the Iron Curtain,* authors Sheila Ostrander and Lynn Schroeder relate that Jacque Errera, Councillor on Nuclear Matters to the Belgian Government, recently became involved in work with a healer who held his hands over a piece of fresh meat. After this "treatment" by the healer the meat apparently was preserved and did not deteriorate for a month even though it was not refrigerated.

Some scientists believe there is a link between the energy body and the Chinese practice of acupuncture, a system of medication that effects cures with needles. According to the theories accompanying acupuncture, the vital energy circulates through the body on specific routes

It can be tapped at several hundred places on the skin, and the Chinese insert fine needles at these points to correct imbalances in the energy flow. John Hersey in his book *Hiroshima* reported that acupuncture can cure the effects of radiation. A large number of American medical doctors, osteopaths, and chiropractors are now using acupuncture and it is under intensive study by medical societies, associations, and academies.

The energy flow from a telepathic message affects the blood volume of the receiver, according to research conducted by Dr. Douglas Dean at the Newark College of Engineering, New Jersey. The investigation was made with a plethysmograph which unerringly measures the blood volume in the thumb. And research at Rosary Hill College in Buffalo, New York, by Sister Justa Smith reveals that the mind can affect enzymes.

Projection of an energy force also is revealed in the strange ability of Ted Serios of Chicago, Illinois, to project an image of his thoughts on Polaroid film. In carefully controlled experiments by Dr. Jule Eisenbud, associate clinical professor of Psychiatry at the University of Colorado Medical School, Serios has produced hundreds of pictures on film by strenuous concentration of his mind. The force he directs toward the film is believed to be the same controlled energy used by Mrs. Mikhailova, Geller, et al, in the movement of physical objects.

The universal nature of the energy field, indicating that it is shared by all living things, is born out by the unusual experiments of Cleve Backster, founder of the Backster Research Foundation in New York. A recognized expert with the polygraph, Backster demonstrated with a number of carefully planned experiments that plants respond to the thoughts, emotions, and actions of people and animals around them. Death of living things, such as shrimp or fish, occurring in the vicinity of the plants produced an intensive reaction on the polygraph. "It seems to indicate some sort of primary perception or consciousness in every living cell," Backster reported. Backster's experiments have now been duplicated and confirmed by Dr. Marcel Vogel, senior chemist at IBM in San Jose, California, and by a host of home experimenters, including ourselves. The experiments with plants will be more fully described in Chapter Four, "Pyramids & Plant Power."

A summary of reports reveals the "new" energy can be refracted, reflected, polarized, and combined with other energies, and produces effects similar to electricity, magnetism, heat, and luminous radiations and, yet, is in itself none of these.

Pyramid research to date reveals some evidence that the space within the Great Pyramid and its smaller replicas enhances, intensifies, and/or generates energy of the electromagnetic spectrum and other forms or degrees of the so-called universal energy. As we will describe in following chapters, the activity within the pyramid form apparently parallels a wide range of paranormal phenomena: the treatment of water by healers and the subsequent effects on treated plants; water treated by the Brown cells —isolated cells containing light-sensitive pigments, particles of crystallized light—and given to plants and animals, and also showing a purification process according to laboratory tests; healing and increase of body energy similar to claims made for Eeman screens, wet- and dry-cell appliances, multiwave oscillator, orgone energy accumulators, etc.; psychic healing and enhancement of transcendental states as described in metaphysical literature as occurring when a guru or teacher raises the energy level of a student.

In the scientific research conducted by Dr. Luis Alvarez, who won the Nobel Prize in physics in 1968, of the Great Pyramid energy fields, standard scientific principles were used. The idea was that cosmic rays passing through the Pyramid would reveal any chambers that had not been found. A cosmic particle recording device would show less loss of energy on passage through a hidden room than it would through solid stone. This research involved several institutions as well as governmental agreement between both the United States and Egypt.

Magnetic tapes, which recorded the data, were run through the most modern computer to analyze the results. According to one of Dr. Alvarez's colleagues, the tapes revealed that a pattern could not be established from which to determine a stable zero point of reference, and every time the tapes were re-run, they gave a different pattern of readings. Not only were the particles different, but certain data disappeared from the tapes. The final conclusion was that what was occurring was not only impossible, but some energy was being registered that does not conform to the laws of science.

According to George W. Van Tassel, director of the Ministry of Universal Wisdom, Inc., the maximum energy to be generated requires 28 days or one magnetic month. Van Tassel claims that a quartz crystal peak on the top, where the capstone would be on the Gizeh pyramid, will produce enhanced effects, and that a laminated quartz condenser, with germanium separating the quartz sheets, on top of the pyramid will produce energy readings on existing scientific equipment.

The stones in the Great Pyramid weigh as much as seventy tons. Granite was used to encase the King's Chamber reputedly because granite produces a piezoelectric effect due to the matrix of quartz crystals, mica, and feldspar. The bulk of the pyramid of Gizeh is limestone, which has no electrical properties. The granite chambers above the King's Chamber are believed by some to form a granite air condenser for energy storage.

"Orgone energy" was the name given by Dr. Wilhelm Reich to what he believed was the primordial, mass-free cosmic life energy in which we and everything on our planet are immersed. The "oraccu" was invented by Reich to allegedly collect and accumulate the life energy in the atmosphere and make it usable for scientific and medical purposes. Reich claimed that orgone energy is able to penetrate everything, but at varying speeds, and while present everywhere, it varies considerably in concentration and quality.

Reich discovered that organic matter (wood, cotton, wool, etc.) readily absorbs orgone energy, whereas metallic matter first absorbs but then repels the energy rapidly. Thus was born the fundamental principle governing the construction of the oraccu devices.

The basic oraccu is a simple six-sided box, all walls of which are constructed in exactly the same manner. The outermost layer of each wall is constructed of organic material, such as wood or pressed composition board. The inner, metallic layer can be made of sheet iron or iron wire mesh (screening). Attention should be paid to both the absorbing (organic) and repelling (metallic) layers, as to the amount and type of materials to be used. For medical and scientific purposes, Reich recommended iron as the best metallic material. Other metals, for example aluminum, he considered harmful for medical purposes. Organic materials vary also in their ability to absorb energy as well as moisture.

The specific layering of organic outer wall and metallic inner wall constitutes a "one-fold" oraccu. Some experimenters have built and used oraccu devices up to ten folds for experimental purposes on plants; however, Reich warned against using an oraccu stronger than three-folds for medical purposes without proper medical supervision.

The layering of organic and metallic walls allegedly establishes a direction of flow of orgone energy from the outside to the inside of the oraccu, where the orgone is concentrated above the level in the surrounding atmosphere. Orgone energy flows from the weaker potential to the stronger potential (just the opposite of electrical flow). Thus the human being within the oraccu attracts the energy to his own orgonotic system, which is higher in potential than the oraccu.

Science has shown that the nucleus of every atom is surrounded by negatively charged particles called electrons, and there may be as few as one and as many as 92 electrons. The electrons whirl around the positively charged nucleus at 186,300 miles per second.

A charged piece of mass whirling around in a circle at the speed of light generates electromagnetic radiation. From every atom there is electromagnetic radiation of extremely short wavelengths, varying from one milli-micrometer to 100 milli-micrometers or more. Every individual atom of every element has its own combination of frequencies being generated continuously.

An excellent statement of the theory is made in Sir William Ramsey's *Physical Chemistry:* "The radiation field itself is produced in the following manner. An electro-magnetic wave or disturbance starts out from a vibrating electrically polar unit—an atomic or molecular system with a special separation of unlike electrical charges—whose vibration involves a periodic fluctuation of its electrical moment. The frequency of the radiation emitted is identical with that of the oscillator itself; its phase, intensity, and state of polarization of the oscillator. If on the other hand, an electrically polar unit is placed in a radiation field the frequency of which approximates to the natural frequency of vibration of the polar unit, the latter will be induced to vibrate in sympathy with the electric vector of the field and energy will be continuously absorbed from the field."

Dr. Robert A. Millikan, former president of the California Institute of Technology and Nobel Prize winner in physics for his work of weighing the electron, speaking before a joint meeting of the technical societies in Kansas City, Missouri, made the following statement: "Some day we will find that each of the elements of material matter vibrates at a frequency, each different from the other."

Dr. I. I. Rabi of Columbia University won the American Association for the Advancement of Science Prize for his work on nuclear resonance. From the *Science News Letter* of January 6, 1940, we find him stating, "Atoms can act like little radio transmitters broadcasting on ultra short waves."

In an interview with the Associated Press, on December 30, 1939, Dr. Rabi said: "Man himself as well as all kinds of supposedly inert matter constantly emit rays. Every atom and every molecule in nature is a continuous radio broadcasting station. Those who believe in telepathy, second sight, and clairvoyance, have in today's announcement the first scientific proof of the existence of invisible rays which really travel from one person to another."

Dr. Flanagan, in the pamphlet mentioned earlier, stated: "The Pyramid of Gizeh generates millimicrowave or nanowave radiation by the simple fact that you have five corners. We have the four base corners and the apex. These corners are in effect a type of nanowave radiator. The radiation from the molecules or the atoms of matter in the Pyramid combine by the angles of the corners into a beam which bisects the angles of the corners and transmits a beam of this radiation towards the center of the Pyramid."

Dr. Flanagan added: "These energies all combine in the center or King's Chamber area of the Pyramid. The molecules or atoms in this area absorb these energies by resonance. As the energy increases, the electron orbits start to expand. As more energy is absorbed, more expansion occurs. There would be a point at which, if there were too much energy absorbed, that the atoms would disintegrate and the electrons would fly off, but the energy required would be far more than the Pyramid could concentrate. As the energy increases, there is an increase in circulation and finally we have a highly saturated energy atmosphere in the wave bands around ten nanometers. These energies also radiate outwards from the corners of the Pyramid."

This energy, known and unknown, would appear to be the matrix of all living things, linking man with man, and man to the cosmos. That the ancient builders of the Great Pyramid understood the nature of this energy and how to use it, remains to be proved perhaps, but the evidence continues to grow that the Great Pyramid (and its miniature progeny being born in home and laboratory) is by either design or by accident—amongst other things—a multi-force field generator.

4. PYRAMIDS & PLANT POWER

He knelt at the edge of an old buffalo wallow where the small prairie flowers grew half-hidden in the bluestem grass of the Kansas Flinthill cattle country. He carefully ran his fingers over the white petals. "These little brothers can mirror your soul. They watch you pass and tell the Great Spirit how your foot falls upon the earth."

"You know of Cleve Backster's experiments with plants, his measurement of their emotional reactions?" Shul asked.

He shook his head but for several moments did not answer as his eyes appeared to contemplate a clump of sumac a short distance away. "Yes," he finally said. "The white man has his ways and it has taken him a long time to discover what the Indian has always known—life is one and you cannot separate it. Form means nothing. Man begins to communicate with himself and others the day he learns that plants, too, share the universal consciousness."

56

The occasion was the 1971 Interdisciplinary Conference on the Voluntary Control of Internal States of Awareness sponsored by the Menninger Foundation. Several of us had taken a break from the sessions to follow Rolling Thunder, chief medicine man of the Shoshone Indian Nation, on a walk through the surrounding meadow. He had been invited to the conference to share with scientists from several countries some of the great and ancient traditions of the Indian medicine man. How often I have thought of him since in our work with plants and when I read of some discovery in man's newfound relationship with plants. I imagine, then, Rolling Thunder reading of the same breakthroughs and a quiet enigmatical smile reflecting a trace of patient amusement.

Perhaps it is the unexpected contact with someone like Rolling Thunder—a voice out of the past and the keeper of an ancient body of knowledge—but we are reminded that we only discover what is already known to at least one intelligence greater than our own. If the Indian medicine man could know, how far back in the chronology of his teachers could one trace this wisdom? These thoughts have a way of creeping in particularly when we search for insights within a structure long known to man. Watching our plants perform what to us was a new ritual within their pyramid confines, we struggled to read in these movements the clues to the ancient knowledge of energy fields.

Considerable evidence is now pointing to plants as one of the keys. Few occurrences in the scientific arenas of recent years have created greater excitement, awe, and an elevation of consciousness than have the experiments with plants. Our examinations of plants growing in pyramids offered some thought-provoking phenomena. What really launched the use of plants as subjects for the new study of energy fields and even consciousness in recent years, however, was a piece of innocent enough research on the morning of February 2, 1966, that completely turned around our concepts of life forms. On that day Cleve Backster, a polygraph expert and former interrogation expert with the CIA, discovered that plants demonstrate an emotional response similar to that in humans.

Endeavoring to measure the rate at which water rose in a plant from the root into the leaf, Backster attached the electrodes of a modified polygraph to the leaves of a dracaena house plant. The polygraph, or lie detector, measures the change in people's breathing, blood pressure, pulse activity, and perspiration caused by emotional stimuli. The change in perspiration is known as galvanic skin response or psychogalvanic reflex (PGR). The results are revealed on the polygraph's strip chart by a pen that makes lines on paper according to the electrical activity of the subject.

Backster reasoned that when the water arrived in the plant's leaf, the resistance would go down and the tracing would go up. The opposite occurred. A study of the chart revealed a tracing typical of a human emotionally aroused. How can a plant have emotional responses? Intrigued, Backster decided to try the threat-to-well-being principle by burning the leaf of the plant with a match. At the instant he thought of lighting the match, there was a dramatic change in the PGR tracing. He was several feet away from the plant and had not even lighted the match and yet the pen was dancing all over the strip chart.

Following up on the threat-to-well-being approach, Backster dropped some brine shrimp into boiling water. Once again the plant showed great agitation. He wondered if cells are able to broadcast some kind of distress signals to other living cells. A carefully planned scientific approach was called for.

Backster determined that he could avoid the possibility of human error by automating his experiments. He constructed machinery that was programmed to kill the shrimp on a random basis, with the timing precisely recorded by the machines. No human remained on the premises. Top scientists agreed that the system could not be faulted.

Electrodes were attached to three separate plants in separate rooms and away from the area where the shrimp would be killed by automatically being dumped in scalding water. The polygraph readings revealed that the emotional response from the plants occurred at the exact instant of the shrimps' death. This experiment has since been repeated many times by Backster and others, all using sophisticated randomizers, programmers, mechanized devices, and the results have always been the same. Equal results have been obtained by damaging or destroying other life forms while monitoring plant reactions to the events. We informally confirmed the threat-to-well-being tests at the Menninger Foundation, and later with a modified polygraph in our garage laboratory.

Backster found that the undefined sensory system or perception capability in cell life could not be blocked by a Faraday screen (which prevents electric penetration) or by lead shields. The signal continued, initiated, it seemed, by a force beyond our electrodynamic spectrum.

Serving with Backster on the advisory council of the Ernest Holmes Research Foundation, we had the opportunity to visit with him recently. He told us that the force appeared to be an unsuspected life signal that quite possibly might connect all creation. His working hypothesis is that all life forms are connected through consciousness at the cellular level—that plants as well as people and animals can communicate with each other on a much higher level than any form of telepathy now known.

Distance is apparently no barrier. A friend's house plant was left with Backster and he discovered that the plant became highly excited when its owner was placed under stress during the landing of her plane in Cincinnati. Backster has since kept an accurate log with a stopwatch whenever he is absent from his laboratory in New York. His moments of excitement, stress, etc., coincide with the polygraph tracings of his plants. Regardless of how far away he is, when he thinks of returning to his office, the plants respond with excitement. It is interesting to note that plants not only show fondness for those who care for them but also fear of strangers and those who have damaged them. Backster tested this point a number of times by playing the role of the "good guy" and having his assistant, Bob Henson, play the role of the villian. Whenever Backster cut his finger or otherwise hurt himself while working in his laboratory, his plants would respond with great sympathy.

In short, Backster's experiments have provided evidence that plants—though believed to be without nerves—register fear, apprehension, relief, and pleasure. But nearly three-quarters of a century ago India's foremost physical scientist, Sir Jagadis Chandra Bose, stated, "Love, hate, joy, fear, pleasure, pain, excitability, stupor, and countless other appropriate responses to stimuli are as universal in plants as in animals."

Dr. Bose's statement was not one of idle speculation. The first Indian to win international distinction in physics, psychology, and physiology, he demonstrated that the plant kingdom is alive with sensibility through the use of his Crescograph—designed to measure and record nervous impulses in animals—which revealed that the plant exhibits excitatory response to mechanical stimulation and undergoes physiological changes identical to those in animal tissue. Using his Resonant Recorder, which measured the speed of transmission of excitatory response, and the Oscillating Recorder, which registered the pulsations of the Telegraph plant, Bose demonstrated the similarity between plant impulses and the pulse beat of the animal heart.

Bose showed that when a plant was pricked with a pin, its growth rate was immediately depressed to a fourth and that it took about two hours for the plant to recover. He demonstrated that a feeble electric stimulus caused a positive change in the pulvinus (it behaves much like a contractile muscle in an animal) of a plant and that a strong stimulus induced a negative electric change. He considered the positive tone to be pleasant to the plant and the negative to be unpleasant or painful.

In his *Autobiography of a Yogi,* Paramahansa Yogananda relates how he watched Bose jab a sharp instrument through a section of a fern. Looking at the fern shadow on the Crescograph's screen, which could magnify impulses 10 million times, he saw the fern tremble spasmodically at the instant of injury and then saw it die, trembling violently, as Bose sliced through the stem. According to Yogananda, the death contraction in the plant appeared to be similar in every respect to the death contraction in the animal.

Bose's Resonant Cardiograph measured infinitesimal pulsations in plants, animals, and humans at the rate of one-hundreth part of a second. According to Patrick Geddes, a professor of botany who wrote *The Life and Work of Sir Jagadis C. Bose,* Dr. Bose developed the cardiograph in the hope that the instrument would lead to vivisection on plants instead of animals.

The power of prayer in plants has been demonstrated many times. Perhaps the most complete research in this area has been accomplished by Reverend Franklin Loehr who founded the Religious Research Foundation of America for this purpose. His three-year experiment in which 150 persons did over 700 unit experiments and made more than 100,000 measurements, demonstrated that prayer can affect the health and growth of plants. His results were published in the bestseller, *The Power of Prayer on Plants.*

Having read of the Loehr experiments, Dr. Robert Miller, an Atlanta chemical engineer and former professor at Georgia Institute of Technology, determined to examine the power of long-distance prayer on plants. He used a rotary electro-mechanical transducer and strip chart recorder in order to measure plant growth. Drs. Ambrose and Olga Worrall, well-known healers, were asked to pray for the plants from their home in Baltimore, some six hundred miles away. During an 11-hour period, the plants grew at the rate of 52.5 mils per hour —over 800 percent the normal rate.

Dr. Bernard Grad, biochemist and professor of psychiatry at McGill University in Montreal, has become internationally known for his experiments with the effects of "laying on of hands," and particularly the telekinetic effect on plant growth. Having found a highly skilled healer in the person of Oskar Estebany, a former colonel in the Hungarian army, Grad spent seven years investigating the nature of Estebany's power. Experiments included having the healer hold seeds in his hands for several minutes prior to planting and holding a container of water that was then poured on experimental groups of seeds. In each case the "treated" seeds had a higher rate of germination and outgrew the untreated seeds.

These experiments would seem to bear out the old adage of the "green thumb" that some people seem to have a knack of growing plants. Luther Burbank stated a half century ago, ". . . one person will plant a flower, attend it carefully, and it will wither. But under identical physical care, a second person may develop the same flower into a healthy thriving plant. The secret . . . is love."

The question immediately becomes how a plant can respond to love unless it can feel? Does the expression of love or caring generate some yet unknown energy force to which the plant responds? Clearly, the above experiments demonstrate that some unknown and invisible force can change the behavior of the plants, sometimes drastically.

The important thing is that when you look at these and other experiments, to be mentioned later in this chapter, in relationship to pyramid research some interesting parallels can be seen. Seeds and plants placed inside pyramid space behave differently than those outside this space.

In our early experiments with plants inside pyramid models, we noticed a significant difference in the growth rate of the experimental plants and the control plants placed outside the pyramids. These observations led us to believe that an energy force captured or generated by the pyramid was affecting the plants. We wondered if this effect could be observed by the use of time-lapse photography.

What we saw—and subsequently showed to a number of scientific and lay observers—were plants gyrating in a symphonic dance as though orchestrated by an unseen conductor.

Our first film showed a sunflower approximately six inches tall, slender, with two well-formed leaves placed at the center of a glass pyramid at the level of the King's Chamber, one-third the distance from the base to the apex. The plant followed an east-west cyclic movement. It bowed to the east nearly touching the base, swept a semicircle to the south and back to the west and finally straightened to the vertical before starting the dance once more. The movement was repeated every two hours according to a block placed beside the plant. Time-lapse photography has since been used a number of times over a period of two years.

For more than two years the east-west movement never changed; always the pattern was the same. Then suddenly in July 1974, the east-west movement stopped and the plants started moving in a north-south arc. We hypothesized that the change might be caused by variations in sunspots or solar flares. Checks with meteorologists and space agencies, which measure these phenomena, failed to provide any clues, however. At this writing, November 1974, the north-south movement continues. We feel certain that the radical change is of some significance and we have even speculated that the plants are monitoring some modification in our environment. We are, of course, continuing our investigation.

Plants outside the pyramids fail to show the gyrations of those inside. Time-lapse photography reveals the plants to be "wallflowers" avoiding the dance of their apparently charged-up peers within the pyramids.

Our experiments seem to indicate that there is some sort of cosmic wind blowing in from the west. When an aluminum screen is placed on the west side of the plant inside the pyramid space, the plants hesitate in their gyrations and then stop moving entirely until the screen is removed or until they grow above the screen. Only that part above the screen moves, however, with the blocked part seemingly inhibited. As long as the screen remains vertically suspended on the west side of the plant, the plant does not wilt and stays healthy yet strangely suspended in limbo.

Apparently the energy field captured, enhanced, or generated by the pyramid includes some part of the electromagnetic spectrum inasmuch as the presence of the aluminum screen seems to block a force field and suspends plant movement. According to our investigations, aluminum is the only metal that serves as an inhibitor. Aluminum is made by an electrical process and might be thought of as having an electrical substance. Perhaps the aluminum produces a negative field or else serves to block the positive field. Seeds placed in saucers on aluminum foil did not germinate in four days although seeds in identical saucers without the aluminum foil germinated in two days. Once the foil or screen has been left in the pyramid for two weeks or so, it apparently becomes saturated with pyramid energy and no longer serves as an inhibitor. Left outside a pyramid for any length of time, however, the aluminum loses its charge and reverts to its role as an inhibitor.

When a magnet is introduced inside a pyramid, small

plants stop their movement. A magnet placed beside a sunflower six inches tall stopped the plant's gyrations at the base level, although the top of the plant continued to move. When the magnet was removed, the plant resumed the movements from the base of the stem. Mysteriously, when plants are placed under plastic domes, permanent magnets appear to inhibit plant movement anywhere in the pyramid except those directly under the apex. In other words, it would seem that the energy is sufficiently strong at that location to overcome a counter force directed by the magnet.

Remembering Dr. Bose's experience that plants nourished with feeble electrical impulses were healthy and happy whereas plants given higher levels of electrical charge deteriorated, we might hypothesize that the aluminum screens and magnets tend to generate an overdose of electrical charges within the pyramid space already charged by its own field activity. It would seem to be a matter of excess leading to abuse for experiments with magnets placed near plants not contained in pyramid space show an increase in plant growth. Also, we might note that in the case of electro-therapy, recipients are warned that low doses of electricity can be beneficial but high doses can be detrimental.

As regards the generating of known electrical fields, the five open spaces or chambers above the King's Chamber in the Great Pyramid might provide the King's Chamber with a capacitor-like effect and the electrical qualities that go with a capacitor. The granite used in many parts of the pyramid came from Aswan, and has a piezo-electric quality much like quartz.

The behavior of a sunflower—observed by means of time-lapse photography—appeared to be very human in its attraction to gold. A roll of 22-carat gold foil was placed inside the pyramid, and the plant reached way over in order to curl around the foil. It finally swayed back in the opposite direction but not nearly as far as usual and quickly returned to embrace the foil.

Anton Mesmer, greatly influenced by the writing of the sixteenth century physician Paracelsus, believed the plants and stars gave off a subtle and invisible magnetic fluid that influenced man's health and well-being. He referred to this force as "animal magnetism." Following Mesmer's death in 1815, his followers called themselves magnetizers. In 1841 a French scientist and magnetizer, Charles Lafontaine, launched a series of plant experiments in order to determine whether the body magnetism that Mesmer believed he could generate and use for healing could have an effect on lower life forms.

Lafontaine made passes over a dying geranium. Not only did the plant regain life, but it grew larger and bloomed more profusely than other nearby geraniums. Excited by the success of Lafontaine, one of his associates, Dr. Picard, obtained similar results with a peach tree. Other experimenters working with Lafontaine also produced healing of a startling nature with fruit trees and obtained more fruit than from control trees in the same plots.

At the present time Sister Justa Smith, enzymologist and chairperson of the chemistry department of Rosary Hill College in Buffalo, New York, has become deeply involved in studying the effect of the force emanating from a healer's hands on enzymes.

Dr. Smith has demonstrated that magnetic fields increase enzyme activity while ultraviolet light damages it. She is now working with Estebany in the examination of his force field and its effects as compared to a high magnetic field. Using four containers of enzymes, the untreated control vial remains at the same temperature as Estebany's hands; the second vial is held by Estebany for seventy-five minutes; the third vial contains enzymes damaged by ultraviolet light, and Estebany treats this vial the same as the second. The fourth container of enzymes is exposed to a high magnetic field of 8,000 to 13,000 gauss. The magnetic field of the earth has been measured at less than one gauss.

One such experiment was conducted daily for a month, and Dr. Smith discovered a significant increase in the enzyme activity of the treated vials as compared to the controls. The enzymes damaged by ultraviolet light and then treated by Estebany were found to be "healed" and brought back to normal activity. And of considerable significance was Dr. Smith's discovery that the activity of the enzymes in the vial treated by Estebany was the same as the vials subjected to a magnetic field of 13,000 gauss.

The question that Sister Justa Smith is asking is whether the force radiated by Estebany—and similar healers—and the magnetically charged field is the same force that normally promotes healing. She is also serving as director of the Human Dimensions Institute at Rosary Hill that is involved in scientific research of the unknown dimensions of man's potential. One of the projects of the institute is to measure the effects of ESP on plants. It is being conducted by Dr. Douglas Dean, on loan from the Newark College of Engineering. Subjects concentrate on making barley seeds grow, and Dr. Dean has found that students who demonstrate the highest ESP scores are able to grow the largest plants.

That growth and healing are initiated by the same force fields comes as no surprise to anyone, but the question raised by pyramid research is whether the energy apparently available within pyramid space is of the same nature. There is some evidence to indicate that it has similar properties: plant growth, bacterial and enzyme activity, and indications of enhanced healing qualities, described elsewhere in this book.

Most of the literature on pyramids suggests that seeds germinate faster and plants grow faster when placed within pyramids. Max Toth and Greg Nielsen state in their book, *Pyramid Power*, "Horticulturists have found that seeds which were placed inside a pyramid before planting germinate more quickly and produce a stronger, healthier plant in a shorter period of time than did seeds which had not been processed in a pyramid."

Oregon psychosensitive Tenny Hale claims that she left a plant cutting out of water in a pyramid for five days and it remained alive. Taken out of the pyramid and placed in water to root, the cutting died in half an hour.

Several experimenters have reported increased plant growth by treating water in a pyramid for a week or more before using it to water house plants.

We have had excellent results with tomatoes by growing them in the pyramid for two weeks before planting outside. These particular tomatoes far outproduced an equal number of control plants. One plant in fact had more than 100 tomatoes on it at one time. Another group of tomatoes did well for a time after being started in a pyramid. Later bugs attacked them, so we placed a flat frame covered with galvanized screen on top of a metal pole and drove it into the ground near one of the plants in the hopes that it would generate a magnetic field around the plant. It grew to more than nine feet tall and produced tomatoes eight feet from the ground. In the meantime, the remainder of the plants died.

But the results are not always consistent. As with other types of experiments, erratic patterns occasionally developed and opposing results sometimes were obtained from identical experiments and where all variables remained the same. For instance, seeds do not always germinate inside pyramids and sometimes they germinate slower than control plants on the outside.

In one experiment we took four trays and put two seeds each of lima beans, pinto beans, and sunflower or folded paper napkins. One tray was moistened with ordinary tap water, one with D-cell water (D-cells are discussed elsewhere in the book), one with pyramid water and one tray was moistened with tap water and placed within the field of the multiwave oscillator for one minute. The seeds treated by the MWO germinated and grew three times faster than the seeds in the other trays. There was little variation in the germination and growth rate of the seeds in the other trays.

Several people have asked us about the advisability of building greenhouses in the pyramid shape. We have suggested that additional research should be done before they invest. While plants often thrive inside pyramids, sometimes they do not. Several verbinias placed in pyramids at various times quickly expired in each case. We have found that toadstools last but a very short time. Tomatoes placed in ground which formerly served as bases for outside pyramids always died. Now and then a plant within a pyramid will stop growing and remain that way for days as though suspended in time.

It might be hypothesized that the reason plants sometimes do much better and occasionally worse inside pyramids or when treated by pyramid water depends upon the amount of beneficial energy present or generated. When plants are retarded or die, it may be the result of too great an electrical charge or, possibly, due to the presence of negative energy of some nature. It has been shown that a feeble electrical current will enhance growth and a strong charge inhibit growth as mentioned, and our experiment with germinating seeds treated by the MWO would seem to confirm this.

Nor are all locations within the pyramid equal. While we anticipated that the growth might occur maximally when the plant was placed at the location of the King's Chamber, this did not prove to be the case. In every instance, the plant closest to the apex of the pyramid had the fastest growth rate. These observations seemed to strengthen existing theories that energy flows up and out the apex of the pyramid.

The literature of the Great Pyramid abounds with references to feelings of electrical charge or the presence of a high energy field while standing on top of the huge structure. Those who have had this experience have recorded their reactions in a variety of ways, from feeling "so highly charged that I imagined myself to be a beacon of light," to "I felt so consumed by the energy field that I had to climb down or lose my senses." Yet, there have been those who have made the climb and mentioned only the view from the top. Occasionally there are references to seeing an aura around the top of the Great Pyramid or an illumination at the summit. Several clairvoyants have reported feeling a flow of energy from the apex of pyramid models. One evening while aligning a pyramid on the north-south axis with a compass, we found that when the compass was held above the apex the needle swung in wild erratic ways. Steadying the compass on top of the structure failed to quiet the needle. But attempts to duplicate this behavior have produced only minor movements of the needle or not at all.

Planes have been warned not to fly over the pyramids because of the upward flowing rays from the apex. It has been reported by pilots flying over the structures that instruments go awry.

If the Great Pyramid was constructed to produce an energy flow to and beyond the apex, one wonders toward what object the energy was directed. How does the quality and quantity of this energy differ from that produced in the King's Chamber or other parts of the Pyramid? The answers to these and many other questions that come to mind must rest with investigations yet to be carried out.

The late Verne L. Cameron of Riverside, California researched pyramid shapes more than twenty years ago. One of the drawings in his personal notebook showed a flow of energy through the pyramid upward through the apex.

In order to measure the differences, if any, of plant growth in various locations of the pyramid, we decided to run a series of experiments. Each experiment was started by placing 50 sunflower seeds on folded blotting paper. The paper was moistened and placed inside widemouth jars. Moistened paper was placed over the mouth of the jars to admit oxygen. Seeds were allowed to germinate and grow to three-eighths of an inch. The sprouts were then transplanted to one and a quarter inch plastic pots filled with potting soil. The pots were fixed with iron picture wire in order that they could be hung inside the pyramid. Each of the sprouts were watered with five grams of tap water at the time of planting and at 8 A.M. each day of the tests. The following table shows the growth of the plants and Figure 1 shows their respective locations inside the pyramid:

	Start	1st Day	2nd Day	3rd Day	4th Day	5th Day
A	⅜"	1½"	2⅜"	4-1/16"	5-9/16"	7¼"
B	⅜"	15/16"	1"	1⅛"	1⅞"	2½"
C	⅜"	1-5/16"	1⅜"	1⅞"	2-3/16"	3-3/16"
D	⅜"	15/16"	⅞"	1-1/16"	1⅜"	2"
E	⅜"	1"	1-1/16"	1-3/16"	1⅜"	1-7/16"
F	⅜"	5/16"	¾"	1⅛"	1¼"	1⅞"
G	⅜"	7/16"	1¼"	1¾"	2⅛"	2⅞"
H	⅜"	½"	⅝"	1-3/16"	2½"	3-1/16"

It is interesting to note that while the plants at the top grew the fastest, the plants suspended half between the apex and the King's Chamber level grew less than either. The least growth was shown by the plants placed on the floor of the pyramid and placed as close as possible to the sides as the slant would permit.

All plants were placed in a plane extending across the pyramid from the center of the south side. So that there would be less possibility of humidity or temperature changes in the various locations in the pyramid, an 18-inch circulating fan was placed ten feet west of the pyra-

mid and another similar fan was placed ten feet east of
the pyramid. Also, a four-inch-square vent hole was
made at the apex of the pyramid.

It well may be that the pyramid is not the best of all
possible shapes in which to grow plants. We had talked
with two experimenters who claimed high rates of plant
growth with the use of cones. We decided to test the pyramid against two other shapes. We constructed one
three-sided with sides slanted at the same degree as the
standard pyramid. The base was nine and three-eighths-
inches square; the sides eight and seven-eighths inches and
an apex height of slightly over six inches. One and a half
inches was removed from the apex to allow a small plastic
pot to be suspended from the top. A cone was constructed of the same material with a base diameter of ten inches
and height of ten inches. Two inches was cut from the top
in order to suspend a pot. The standard pyramid had an
apex height of six inches and one and a half inches was
removed from the top.

Five tests were run on plant growth. The averages were
as follows:

Shape	Plant Height at Start	1st Day	2nd Day	3rd Day	4th Day	5th Day
4-sided	⅜"	1 5/16"	2½"	4 3/16"	5¾"	7¾"
3-sided	⅜"	1¾"	2⅝"	4⅜"	5-11/16"	8⅛"
Cone	⅜"	1 7/16"	2⅜"	4½"	6"	8⅜"

Not only was the growth the greatest with the cone,
second with the three-sided pyramid, and last with the
standard pyramid, but this ranking followed in each of the
tests.

In his notebook, Cameron relates his experiences with
the effects of cones on plant growth.

"Eventually I hung six aluminum closed-base twenty-two inch cones in a big tree behind my home. A single wire bled the energy off the apex of each attached to the base of the next one. This kept the energy in a circuitous route, as each one gathered more energy and fed it into the circuit. The surplus energy was then led down another wire to a common copper mesh kitchen scouring pad.

"At first I used the cones with the bottoms open, but later I discovered that one cone with a thin aluminum sheet covering the bottom was approximately as powerful as the three with open bases. I also found the cone need not be out of doors but could be hung fairly high up on the wall, inside the house.

"The length of the conducting wire is not important (the current is not anxious to leave it). Neither is the wire size important.

"In one case-test I hung a cone on the garden fence and ran the wire to it, and along, under a row of radish seeds—half the length of the row. The seeds not over the buried wire came up normally and grew well, but those planted over the wire nearly all failed. The few surviving plants soon wilted or did not develop." Again, we seem to have an excess of energy affecting negatively the growth of plants. Cameron had used the cones, singly, to produce an increase in the growth rate. It might also be noted that in Cameron's experiments with the series of cones that aluminum material was used.

Wilhelm Reich, who worked with particular energy fields, referred to this energy as "orgone," a cosmic energy that obeys functional rather than mechanical laws. He constructed orgone accumulators known as "oraccus." With these oraccus, Reich and others demonstrated the existence and effects of orgone energy. While the work of Reich is discussed elsewhere in the book, we might note in this chapter on plants that experimenters have reported growing plants rapidly and vigorously in oraccus. The oraccu is generally a six-sided box with all sides made of alternating layers of organic and nonorganic materials. In his book, *The Cancer Biopathy,* Reich notes that "A grass infusion develops no protozoa, or very few, when kept from the beginning in the orgone accumulator. Clearly, orgone energy charges the grass tissue and prevents its disintegration into protozoa."

The study of energy fields partaking of but also lying outside of the electromagnetic spectrum—whether we refer to them as cosmic, pranic, odic, psychotronic, or orgonic—have brought us to a place where we are faced with consciousness below the cellular level. The examination of plants has played an integral role in the investigation of these unknown energies and their expression through emotional and mental channels. There would appear to be a close affiliation between plants and human beings, a relationship that goes far beyond the sharing of chemical substances.

The transfer of energy and the communication between humans and plants has been under close scrutiny by Dr. Marcel Vogel ever since he read of the Backster experiments. Vogel is a senior research chemist with International Business Machines and the recipient of a number of scientific awards. He proved to himself that energy directed by the mind can affect the energy fields of plants by keeping a picked elm leaf alive and green for four weeks by sending it mental energy while a control leaf dehydrated and turned brown in a few days.

Vogel is of the opinion that crystals are brought into a solid state of existence by pre-forms, or ghost images of pure energy that anticipate the solids. As it has been demonstrated that plants pick up intentions from human beings, Vogel concluded that intent produced some kind of energy field.

In the spring of 1971, Vogel initiated experiments in order to establish the exact moment when a plant entered into recordable communication with a human subject. He attached a galvanometer, which produced a straight base line, to a philodendron. He stood in front of the plant, relaxed, breathed deeply, and sent affectionate and loving thoughts toward the plant, much as one might do toward a friend. Each time that Vogel conducted this experiment, a series of ascending oscillations was described on the chart by the pen holder. Vogel stated that during these times he could feel, on the palms of his hands, an out-pouring of energy from the plant.

It may be of some significance to note the parallels be-tween the occasional erratic behavior of plants placed within pyramids and the fact that Vogel discovered that some philodendrons responded faster than others, some more distinctly, and that not only plants but individual leaves demonstrated their own unique behavior. He found that plants go through phases of activity and inactivity, appearing highly energized or excited at times and slug-gish or moody at other times.

"From his own experiences, Vogel knew that masters of the art of Yoga, and teachers of other forms of deep meditation such as Zen, are unaware of disturbing influ-ences around them when in meditative states," Peter Tompkins and Christopher Bird state in *The Secret Life of Plants*. "An electroencephalograph picks up from them quite a different set of brain waves than when the same persons are alert to the everyday world around them. It became clearer to Vogel that a certain focused state of consciousness on his part seemed to become an integral and balancing part of the circuitry required to monitor his plants. A plant could be awakened from somnolence to sensitivity by his giving up his normally conscious state and focusing a seemingly extra-conscious part of his mind on the exact notion that the plant be happy and feel loved, that it be blessed with healthy growth. In this way, man and plant seemed to interact, and, as a unit, pick up sensations from events, or third parties, which became re-cordable through the plant. The process of sensitizing both himself and the plant, Vogel found, could take only a few minutes or up to a half hour.

"Asked to describe the process in detail, Vogel said that first he quiets the sensory responses of his body organs, then he becomes aware of an energetic relationship between the plant and himself. When a state of balance between the bioelectrical potential of both the plant and himself is achieved, the plant is no longer sensitive to noise, temperature, the normal electrical fields surrounding it, or other plants. It responds only to Vogel, who has effectively tuned himself to it—or perhaps simply hypnotized it."

Serving with Vogel on the Advisory Committee of the Ernest Holmes Research Foundation (the same committee on which Backster serves), I (Schul) had the opportunity to visit with him one evening about his experiments. "I believe we have demonstrated that man can communicate with plant life," he told me. "Plants are sensitive, living objects. While they may not see or hear in the human sense, they are sensitive instruments for measuring man's emotions. Plants radiate energy which is beneficial to man, and vice versa."

The above statement would agree with Rolling Thunder's contention that the Indian understands the energy fields of various plants and trees. When in need of a physical or energy lift, the Indian would either embrace the pine tree or place his back against the tree for several minutes in order to replenish his power. It is interesting to note that New York psychiatrist John C. Pierrakos, who has tabulated the energy pulsations of humans and plants, states that the pulsatory energy field around spruce and pine trees is between 18 and 22 times a minute and paralleling closely the 15 to 25 pulsations per minute of the average person.

Explaining the pulsatory movements in a monograph entitled, "The Energy Field in Man and Nature," Pierrakos stated:

". . . But what are those inner pulsatory movements? They are the sum total of the processes of life; of all the energies of the metabolism of life within this body. This sum total of energies within this body, also flows out of this body, in the same manner as a heat wave travels out of an incandescent metal object. They create an energy field made up of lines of force in the periphery of his organism. Man's body lives within this energy field which extends several feet away in the immediate vicinity, and at times can be seen traveling several dozen feet out of himself. . . . Living organisms are able to emit light through the entire surface of their bodies; they have not lost their ability to luminate. This phenomena constitutes the energy field, or Aura, which is, in effect, a reflection of the energies of life processes."

In the section, "The Energy Field of Plants and Crystals," Dr. Pierrakos explained:

"As for its nature, it is very sensitive and responds to emotional and physical states and has specific characteristics in illness and health. People affect each other's energy field since the field constantly surrounds us and contacts the field of the neighboring person or groups of people. We are living in each other's field when we are in close proximity. The field pulsates from 15-25 times a minute in man at rest, and extends several feet away from the periphery of the body. The physical body mirrors what is happening in the energy field. The physical body seems to reflect the state of the energy field which shows, many times, the pathological changes which become structural at a later date in the organs and tissues."

Later on in the same section he states:

"From my observations of the energy field of leaves, I noticed that the orientation of the plant to the geographic cardinal points is related to the number of pulsations that each leaf emits. For example, in a white snowball plant, the leaves pointing to the south pulsate 28 times a minute, those to the north 32 times a minute, and those pointing to the west and east also pulsate approximately 28 times a minute. Changing the position of the plant disturbs this pattern of pulsation. This was first pointed out in the work done by George and Marjorie de la Warr. Following their work, I positioned plants in different directions and found it to be true. The plant will orient itself towards the geographic cardinal points and, depending on the species of the plant, there is a different pulsatory rate of the parts of the plants that point in these directions. After a period of time, the leaves rotate and the plant acquires a new orientation, commensurate with its nature and needs, in order to exchange its energy with the atmosphere. The energy field pulsates outwardly, into the surrounding air, for approximately 2 to 4 seconds. Following this, there is a reversal of movement and the energy of the surrounding air streams into the plant. I believe that this may play an important part in the process of photosynthesis."

These observations by Pierrakos raise some interesting questions as regards experiments with plants in pyramids. It would appear that the energy field within the pyramid alters in some fashion the natural movement of the plants, judging from the accentuated gyrations. This being the case, it would seem to follow that the pulsations of the different parts of the plant would also be altered. The question then becomes are the movements of the plants within the pyramid efforts to orient themselves on cardinal points? Would monitoring the plants by means of the polygraph reveal "confusion" or "distress" on the part of the plants in their efforts to "find themselves" in this new energy field? Pierrako's findings were based on observations of the pulsations of the plant's aura. Would Kirlian photography, taking pictures of the plant's aura or electrical field while inside the pyramid, reveal an increased or enhanced energy field? Would the difference between the normal field and the increased field provide us with one way of measuring the energy captured or generated by the pyramid? Further, following Pierrakos's lead that different plants have different pulsatory rates, if the above measurement could be made of a plant with the same pulsation as a human, could we assume that a human subject would experience the same energy increase? While one might raise the question as why not simply measure the electrical output of a human subject inside and outside a pyramid, the problem might be in eliminating such variables as expectation, anxiety, etc. A sufficient number of measurements, however, should allow the experimenters to deal with these variables. For that matter, in view of the Backster and Vogel investigations, the researcher cannot ignore these emotions in plants, either indigenous to the plant or due to monitoring of human responses. In any case, if something is going on inside the pyramid which is not going on outside it, either clairvoyant observations or Kirlian photographic measurements of plant or human auras might be a step toward a greater understanding of the pyramid's energy force field. Aside from the above questions, since plants evidently endeavor to orient themselves on the cardinal points and since it is important to align pyramids along the north-south and east-west axis, would radical changes in the movements of the plants indicate changes in the cosmic rays reaching our atmosphere, sunspot and solar flare activities, possibly even movements of the earth's axis?

Vogel would lead us to believe that it would be extremely difficult to measure the behavior of plants without taking into consideration the human equation. Tompkins and Bird quote Vogel as saying: "It seems that I act as a filtering system which limits the response of a plant to the outside environment. I can turn it off or on, so that people and plant become mutually responsive. By charging the plant with some energy within me, I can cause the plant to build up a sensitivity for this kind of work. It is extremely important that one understand that the plant's response is, in my opinion, not that of an intelligence in plant form, but that the plant becomes an extension of oneself. One can then interact with the bioelectric field of the plant, or through it, with the thought processes and emotions in a third person.

"Vogel concluded that a Life Force, or Cosmic Energy, surrounding all living things is sharable among plants, animals, and humans. Through such sharing, a person and a plant become one. 'This oneness is what makes possible a mutual sensitivity allowing plant and man not only to intercommunicate, but to record these communications via the plant on a recording chart.' "

Pierrakos uses plants to monitor the physical and mental health conditions of his patients. Without calling attention to his observations, the psychiatrist watches the responses of his house plants, the pulsations of their auras, to help determine his diagnostic evaluations. The plants, it seems, pick up the pulsations of the patients, increasing or decreasing their pulsations accordingly.

Vogel and Backster seem to be saying that the human being is at the heart of the universe, that we cannot decipher what is occurring to any other form—mineral, plant, animal—with the human component dismissed from the observation. Within this model, man is an integral part of all natural phenomena. Investigations that fail to include the human integral cannot be other than incomplete or distorted.

To what extent, then, are plants monitoring the world beyond their immediate selves and, further, how and to what extent does the human play in this patterning?

Could it be that the very act of placing a plant within a pyramid, this paying of attention, is in itself a request of the plant to mirror certain conditions that are primarily applicable to the human construct? Was this the intent of the builders of the Great Pyramid? Are plants endeavoring somehow to deliver this message?

5.   EFFECTS ON LIQUIDS

When Ponce de Leon searched for the fountain of youth,
it was evident that he believed that somewhere in those
Florida pines was a quality of water different from the
stuff he was getting back home.

Was Ponce de Leon considered peculiar or senile by
his contemporaries? Not at all. Whereas not everyone believed as he did, it was not unusual for 16th century Europeans to believe that there were secrets of nature which
if discovered could maintain and prolong life. They were
steeped in the legends of antiquity that told them that
greater races in the past had once held these secrets.
Their religions—including Christianity—taught them that
man had once lived to several hundred years but had become corrupt and contaminated. The alchemists amongst
them searched diligently for the formulas and no doubt
perennially told their financial backers that breakthroughs
were imminent.

And today? The legends live on; the theologians still

espouse from the pulpits a better and cleaner way of life and the alchemists in our laboratories throughout the land are still searching for the nectar, in liquid, pill, or capsule, which will refresh our youth and renew our vigor.

A quixotic syndrone? An empty, impossible dream? Who can answer beyond an opinion? The point really is that man believes that there are answers to be found and he gives expression to that faith each time he peers into a microscope or strains for another piece of space with his telescope. Man is a believer and perhaps, in the final analysis, he himself creates the world he believes in.

So, the dream is current. Today excitement is being generated by some unusual phenomena created by putting containers of water, as well as other liquids, within pyramid replicas and watching the results. We have provoked some of the excitement by getting some interesting results from our experiments, by publicizing them, via newspaper, radio, and television, and encouraging others to conduct their own experiments. Other experiments with the B-cells and the multiwave oscillator have contributed their share of excitement. They will be described briefly in this chapter and at greater length in later chapters.

Briefly, water and other liquids have been treated in pyramids, as well as by other methods, and results have either been detected in the liquid itself or in the recipient of the liquid. These results as measured by us or as reported by others include the purification of water, body changes as subjectively monitored and as observed by others, increased plant growth, enhanced healing of wounds, remission of disease symptoms, preservation of milk, fruit juice, etc., without chemical additives or refrigeration, and the rapid maturing of wine.

Before describing this research, the specific experiments, and relating the results, we would like to call the reader's attention to what well may be an important ye little known area of research in the field of chemistry. It needs to be mentioned here because it seems to establish in part a scientific basis for the phenomena to be described.

The theory of biological transmutations contends that certain chemical substances can be changed into other substances. This disputes chemical laws as now generally understood. Lavoisier, the father of modern chemistry, established the principle that nothing is lost, nothing is created, everything is transformed. The atom was considered the smallest particle of matter, a constant in nature, and it was assumed that no element could be created. The atom could not disappear. If it separated from a molecule of two or more atoms, it would be found unchanged in another molecule.

The Lavoisier principle could not be refuted, nor was it even open to debate. It was the basis for the science of the 19th century. It was not until this century that this principle was to experience its first officially recognized contradiction. This was Marie Curie's discovery of natural radioactivity, revealing that some substances can be transmuted into different substances, a concept for which the alchemists of the Middle Ages were to be later ridiculed. An atom of radium was transformed into a non-radioactive and stable atom of lead.

In 1959 a French chemist, Louis C. Kervran startled the field of chemistry with publication of his book, *Biological Transmutations*. In his epilogue, Kervran stated: "The preceding pages have demonstrated that the biological transmutations of the elements do not in any way oppose the laws of chemistry. Chemistry is the science of the displacement of the electrons situated in the peripheral layers of the atoms. It is the science of the molecule, not of the nucleus of the atoms. . . . The phenomenon that I have unveiled exists at the level of the atom's nucleus.

Thus it is a new science, quite different from chemistry which is simply the end result of the transmutation phenomenon and therefore possesses certain limitations."

In the foreword to Kervran's book, Michel Abehsera provides us with some historical background on the subject. He relates that in 1799 the French chemist Vauquelin became curious of the quantity of lime excreted every day by hens and decided to put a hen in a cage and feed it only oats. He measured the amount of lime present in the oats before feeding the grain to the hen. After the grain was eaten, he analyzed the amount of lime excreted through the eggs and fecal matter and discovered that the hen excreted five times more lime than it had eaten in the feed.

In 1822 an Englishman by the name of Prout was the first to clearly define the nature of the transmutation of elements, according to Abehsera. Prout systematically examined the increase of limestone inside an incubating chicken egg, proving that limestone is not contributed by the shell.

In 1831 a Frenchman by the name of Cheubard germinated watercress seeds in an insoluble dish with distilled water and verified that the young plants contained minerals that had not existed in the seeds.

Apparently this research went unnoticed for more than 120 years. Kervran's unveiling, however, has drawn attention in Europe where chemists and other scientists are divided over his findings.

Kervran cites many cases in his book. He contends that the problems of decalcification and the strengthening of bones must be re-investigated, and he points to the rapid healing of bones by means of organic silica. The chief surgeon of a hospital requested Kervran's help when he found himself confronted with a delicate case: a young man with bones broken very badly in an accident. The classical treatment of vitamin D plus phospho-calcic salt formula failed to bring about improvement. Kervran administered organic silica and the bones rapidly healed.

By way of another example, Kervran states that under certain conditions the sodium in the blood can become potassium, and that magnesium and silicon are two of man's principal sources of limestone.

"I remind the reader of the experiments made in the Sahara Desert where for six months petroleum workers excreted an average of 320 milligrams more calcium every day than they ingested, and this without decalcification," Kervran asserts. "All that has been written on the metabolism of calcium which does not take into account the biological transmutations must be studied all over again, as there are important facts medicine must begin to use."

Of Kervran's presentation of his findings, Abehsera stated in the foreword: "Having waited for years, witnessing thousands of convergent analyses, he succeeded in demonstrating that not only molecules but atoms themselves can be transformed. He verified that there is transmutation of matter from one single body to another, from one atom to another. . . ."

If, indeed, A does not always remain A but instead can become B, then we are faced with the need for greater insights as to the nature of chemical substances. Substitution has, then, become part of the chemical ballgame.

The implications of biological transmutations did not miss Abehsera's attention. He stated: "Of special importance is the place they (biological transmutations) will occupy between the scientist and the metaphysician. So far there has never been a direct dialogue between the two, because of the differences in language. Now I believe their meeting is possible, for the biological transmutations teach us about the movement of life. From this movement the scientiest will see that science can no longer limit itself to the study of the physical alone, form movement implies elevation toward the metaphysical, not entrophy. From this same movement, animating the invisible elements, the metaphysician will learn that life is worth studying in the most singular aspects. He will discover in the minute that which he always knew, that life is a continual renewal of self and cell."

Prior to our experiments in the treatment of water we had had some experience with other liquids. Our interest in testing milk was initiated upon learning that two separate milk firms, one in France and the other in Italy, were using cartons in the shape of pyramids after discovering that unrefrigerated milk kept fresher longer than in rectangular-shaped containers.

We obtained a quantity of fresh homogenized milk and filled two identical containers, with loosely crumpled paper placed over the top to reduce the contamination from airborne bacteria. One container was placed inside a pyramid and the other outside with similar light, heat, and air circulation.

Six days later the milk in the pyramid had separated solids with stratified layers of curds or watery liquid, and with a percipitate of what appeared to be powdered calcium. The milk on the outside of the pyramid had separated somewhat, though not to such a noticeable extent, and mold was forming around the top of the milk.

A day later the milk on the outside of the pyramid had a much heavier growth of mold while the milk within the pyramid had even more pronounced stratification of layers. At this time the milk outside was discarded but the milk inside the pyramid was kept in place. Six weeks later the experiment was concluded: the milk had settled into a solid, creamy, smooth substance of what appeared and tasted like yogurt. No mold was apparent; stratification of the layers of solids had combined and were no longer noticeable.

This experiment has been done a number of times since

and with slightly varying results. At times the milk will not change to yogurt but will simply stratify, separating the components of the milk into layers. However, as long as the milk is inside the pyramid it will not develop mold. We have not been able to determine exactly what the difference is between the times when the milk turns to yogurt and when it stratifies. We believe that variations in temperature and humidity have a bearing, although we have tried to keep these constant. Also, we speculate that the seasons, phases of the moon, varying degrees of cosmic radiation, and so on, likely have a bearing on the experiments. Judging from Dr. Alvarez's experiences in measuring cosmic radiation, the energy fields within the pyramid vacillate from time to time for reasons yet unknown.

A chemist in an Oklahoma state agency became interested in the effects of pyramid space on liquids. He attended one of our lectures and after visiting with us on two occasions decided to test the milk.

He made his first test in the agency's laboratory and found no change in the two milk samples. We suggested that perhaps the metal deck roof on the building, and the presence of high frequency currents, 120 and 220 volt equipment, fluorescent lighting, etc., might inhibit the forces within the pyramid.

The chemist then duplicated the test in a frame building, well away from the laboratory, and after ten days found that bacteria had been reduced by 16 percent in the milk placed within the pyramid. He said that had the test period been extended it would no doubt have resulted in a higher figure of bacteria destroyed.

In a letter to the editors of *The Pyramid Guide,* Irwin Trent of Tustin, California reported:

"Once upon a time Mr. Cameron told me about the only cheese experiment he ever made in a pyramid. It lasted 35 days. So I placed some raw milk in glasses under two different size pyramids made of posterboard without bases. In about a week a one-sixteenth inch thick surface developed with a light brownish color on top.

"In two weeks, cheese accumulated underneath it, and a heavy cheese odor was apparent at all times thereafter. After sixty days there were one half inch residues. I dowsed them for fitness and then ate the cheeses. They were delicious! The brown surfaces might have been from the sugar in the milk.

"On another occasion, I placed raw milk, powdered goat's milk solution, and a small glass of raw cream under various pyramids. Up to two weeks, everything was the same as above. Then different colored areas appeared on the surfaces except that of the cream. Gray cobwebs with a gauzy appearance grew upwards. I scraped growths away and tested the cheese underneath. It was okay, so I let the process continue. The different colored areas appeared again. I repeated the scraping. By this time, the natural processes had been ruined. The glass of raw cream was next to another glass with growths which developed normally into rich cream cheese."

Anyone experimenting with liquids should bear in mind that they are not constant from day to day, or even hour to hour. This was explained very well by Michel Gauquelin in his book, *Cosmic Clocks:*

"Only recently has it been understood how constantly present the influences of space are around and within us. A few years ago, no one had any idea why chemical or biological reactions could vary from day to day despite all precautions to the contrary. The fact is, as far as liquids are concerned, there are never any constant conditions. Of course identical laboratory experiments with solids would not give similar results, since the organization of solid systems is almost unmodifiable; weak influences have no effect on it. But solids are not life.

"Life is the unstable equilibrium of the liquid element.

No amount of precaution can shield the unstable structure of liquids from the effects of outside forces. It is not chance but a permanent law of nature that makes experiments with liquids difficult to reproduce from one hour to the next."

Gauquelin tells us of the research done by Professor Giorgie Piccardi, director of the Institute for Physical Chemistry in Florence, into the erratic behavior of water.

Piccardi knew that water leaves calcareous deposits inside containers such as cooking pots and industrial boilers. These chemical deposits act as nearly perfect insulators that greatly reduce the efficiency of the unit. One process has been developed to remove the deposits—the adding of specially treated water to the boiler at regular intervals.

Piccardi prepared the water by stirring a glass containing a drop of mercury and low pressure neon and pouring it in the water to be treated. As the glass container is moved about, an electrical current is created by the mercury rubbing the sides of the container, and this slight charge is such as to cause a red luminescent discharge through the neon gas. When this "activated" water was introduced into the tubes of the boiler, the scales and deposits of chemical coating were magically softened and could be drawn from the tubes as a muddy sludge.

However, Piccardi discovered that this treatment did not work the same at all times. One day the results would be remarkable and on other days the action of the activated water had no more effect than ordinary water. The activiated water was tested by every means possible, but no difference could be found from plain tap water. How could the movement of the neon and mercury effect a change in an unknown manner in the water to which it was subjected?

Piccardi wrestled with the problem of the renegade water for some time, and then came to the conclusion that the water was influenced by some cosmic force. He found that by covering the vials of activated water with metal screens the effect of the water was modified, keeping some forces from entering from the outside. He determined that the behavior of the activated water depended on something happening in the space surrounding the vials.

Piccardi developed a method of testing water so that he could scientifically determine the cause of the errant behavior of water in chemical reactions. He chose, as the chemical reaction portion of the tests, an inorganic celloid, bismuth exychloride. Pouring trichloride of bismuth into distilled water, the chemical dissolves in the water and settles to the bottom of the container.

Making 20 tests daily for nine years, Piccardi confirmed that the chemical reaction time coincided precisely with sunspot activity, reacting quickly when sunspot activity was at a peak, and reacting slowly when sunspot activity was ebbing.

We tested a jar of instant coffee and a bottle of the cheapest wine we could find. An aluminum plate 10 inches in diameter was placed in a pyramid for five weeks. The plate was then removed and the coffee and wine was set on it. The wine was allowed to remain on the plate for two weeks before opening.

We started using the coffee immediately. The longer it remained on the plate the more mellow the coffee tasted. The wine, when opened, was smooth, mellow, and tasted like much more expensive wine. A distinct difference could be noted between it and the untreated bottle of the same wine. Of course, these are subjective tests and one could easily argue that imagination is a factor. However, we tested several subjects on the wine. They were not told they were taking part in an experiment but were simply asked to distinguish between the qualities of the wine. In each instance, they chose the "treated" wine and a remark of one young man was typical: "It doesn't take much of a wine fancier to tell the difference."

It has been known for some time that drops of plain water can act as independent flowing objects. When dropped to the surface of clean water, some of the drops will form perfect spheres and float or roll on the surface of the water subject to the slightest wisp of air.

Experiments were made using plain water and pyramid water, which had been in the force zone of the pyramid for four weeks. Droplets of water were obtained by punching a hole in the bottom of a small metal container. The container was first filled with plain water and held over a pan of plain, clear water. This pan had been filled to the point that the water formed a convex shape, and a meniscus had formed at the rim. When the drops from the can struck the surface of the water in the pan, small spheres were formed. Some remained on the surface and some would flow to the edge and off the surface of the water.

However, when pyramid water was placed in the can, the drops were less consistent in forming small spheres. This seemed to indicate that the molecules of the pyramid water had actually been spread somewhat apart by the pyramid force, thus having the effect of somewhat lessening the surface tension of the water droplet.

Tenny Hale, an Oregon psychic-sensitive, reported that in her experience the water left inside a pyramid somehow retains its oxygen. If the water is frequently removed from the pyramid, there are fewer oxygen bubbles.

Water treated for four weeks inside the pyramid evaporates faster than plain water, according to our measurements. Several tests were run with 250 grams each of pyramid water and plain water and on each occasion the pyramid water lost 21 more grams in a 15-day period than the plain water.

If the molecular structure of the hydrogen and the oxygen of the water has been changed in some fashion by the pyramid forces, it would seem that there would be a difference in the surface tension of the water. This would account for the differences in evaporation.

We conducted several experiments in the germination of seeds with B-cell water, pyramid water, water treated in a multiwave oscillator, and plain water. B-cells are developed from a culture with the alleged ability to radiate solar energy of very high frequencies. The cells are held in a small matrix of concrete. The multiwave oscillator develops radio waves of varying frequency and when the electromotive force is induced in the cell's nucleus, it allegedly raises the cell's metabolic rate.

Equal units of water were treated separately by B-cells, by the multiwave oscillator, and by the pyramid. Two seeds each of lima beans, pinto beans, and sunflowers were placed on paper napkins in metal trays and moistened with the various water samples. The seeds by the water treated by the multiwave oscillator germinated and grew three times faster than the seeds in the other trays.

It has been our experience that while pyramid water helps a plant after it is growing, it tends to slow down germination time. These experiments are described more fully in the chapter on plants.

It is interesting to note a paragraph in an article, "Medical Applications of Magnetism," (*Bulletin of the Atomic Scientists,* October 1972) by Dr. E. H. Frei, Head of the Department of Electronics at Weizmann Institute:

"It has been suggested by Labes that magnetic fields can influence life processes through liquid crystals, which are intermediate phases between the solid and liquid states occurring in many organic compounds. They exhibit appreciable orientation in some directions but also freedom of movement. It is well known that many liquid crystals orient in fields on the order of 1,000 gauss, and it had been shown by Svedberg that in such oriented liquid crystal systems there can be a marked change in diffusion and in rates of chemical reactions in magnetic fields. Liquid crystals and materials that are near to liquid crystals exist in living bodies, and through these materials the rate of life processes could be influenced."

We took a piece of decayed meat and divided it into two equal parts and placed the parts in plain water and pyramid water. After a week, the meat in the untreated water had continued to decay and the odor was quite noxious, and the water was discolored. But the odor from the container of pyramid water was gone, the sediment in the water had precipitated and the water was clear.

We have tried using pyramid water on cuts and burns and believe the healing time is somewhat shortened. For example, a friend's four-year-old daughter mashed her hand and thumb in a slamming door. He started to take her to a doctor but thought of the pyramid water he had kept in his refrigerator. He placed his daughter's hand in the water and after a minute she stopped crying and exclaimed, "Daddy, that feels good." The hand was kept in the water for 30 minutes. The following morning the torn flesh was already starting to grow back together, the swelling was gone, as was most of the discoloration. Two days later there was no sign of the injury.

Mrs. Pettit used pyramid water on her face as a lotion. She found that it stood in beads on her face until absorbed by the skin or until evaporated while untreated water tended to run off in streaks. After bathing her face for some four to five weeks, friends started commenting on her complexion saying, "My, Inez, your complexion is so youthful and clear. What have you been doing?"

We find that a daily glass of pyramid water acts as an aid to the digestive system. An upset stomach will quickly reorganize and elimination seems to be improved.

There are a number of so-called miracle springs in the world with alleged curative powers. When you hear their devotees proclaim the benefits to be gained by bathing and drinking these waters, one cannot help but compare these claims with the results seemingly derived from using pyramid water, as well as water treated by B-cells, multi-wave oscillators, and so on.

In *Health Secrets From Europe* Paavo O. Airola discusses the use of water in treatment and mentions a water treatment clinic in Germany:

"The modern inquiry in balneology (medical science of curing and preventing sickness by bathing) and the medicinal value of mineral waters is recent and as yet incomplete. But what is already known indicates that mineral waters do indeed have curative powers. And they should, inasmuch as disordered mineral metabolism and biochemical derangement are at the root of many diseases. But what is even more important is the fact that these waters here in Bad Pyrment have been used for healing purposes for almost two thousand years; and millions of sick people have been benefited by them—patients and doctors see examples of it every day!"

And the question one finds himself asking is: "Is water, which is so essential to life, the agent for the transference of not only minerals but also known and unknown energy forces to cellular life? Can certain conditions enhance this transference of energy?"

In Christopher Hills's book, *Nuclear Evolution,* we find the following paragraph on the nature of water:

"No movement of electrical energy can take place in living organic life without hydrolysis of water. Life began in water and it appears that the function of the body as a vehicle for the spirit (consciousness) is to make water and hold water for all the protoplasm and its exchange of nutrients. Without this water in each cell there could be no ionisation of the membranes and no activity in the electron pumps, these energy generating wet-cell batteries which we call mitrochendria. As Christ put it, 'Nothing can be born again without spirit and water.' "

Maybe one day soon we will discover that holy water does in actuality possess qualities superior to those of ordinary water. Perhaps water that has been blessed by a nonordinary person takes on additional fields of energy of benefit to its recipients. Perhaps the religious rite of baptism offers more than a symbol of acceptance of purification to the initiate. And just maybe Ponce de Leon was a man ahead of his time.

6. EFFECTS ON SOLIDS

Gold from base metals, the frantic pursuit of the ancient and medieval alchemist, is not one of the accomplishments we can claim for the pyramid. Or is it?

There is something strangely fascinating about alchemy. The better part of its art has been said to be not the Midas touch but the changing of the baseness of man into a god. Some historians believe that the alchemists were master metaphysicians hiding their true purpose of bringing a metamorphosis about in man behind chemical pursuits in order to avoid persecution by religious fanatics. A number of alchemists were subsidized by wealthy patrons who clung to the age-old belief that an elixir produced at the moment of transmutation brought immortality to those who drank it. But whatever the desired goal, alchemy would unveil some deep secret of life. Man cannot help but search for the Philosopher's Stone.

Today's alchemist knows that he is dealing with energy fields and that matter is simply a configuration of energy particles. If he can uncover the secret of nuclear particles, metal can be reconstructed in any fashion desired. While it may have been greed that drove some alchemists, his dreams may not have been as far removed from reality as it might once have seemed. Recent scientific breakthroughs in the investigation of atomic structures have led us to the threshold of understanding the energy matrix in which everything exists. Perhaps the ancients understood this and the alchemist was trying to unravel a forgotten knowledge. Exploration of the effects of the unusual energy fields within pyramids is keeping with this tradition. Today we know that transmutation does occur; a substance can change into another substance.

Lavoisier, a scholar of the 18th century, has been considered the father of modern chemistry. The general principle with which he worked and from which he derived his new science is that nothing is lost, nothing is created, everything is transformed. As the atom was considered the smallest particle of matter and a constant in nature, it was assumed that no element could be created. The atom simply could not disappear. If it separated from a molecule of two or more atoms, it could be found unchanged in another molecule.

This principle of Lavoisier could in no way be refuted; it was not even open to debate. It was the basis for the science of the 19th century. Those who studied it gave it a general extension and applied it to every science corresponding to chemistry. It was not until this century that this principle, which had not been discussed for more than 100 years, was to experience its first officially recognized contradiction. This was the discovery of natural radioactivity, revealing that some substances can be transmuted into different substances. An atom of radium was transformed into a non-radioactive and stable atom of lead as one learned in reading of the work of Marie Curie and her discovery of radium.

Contentions that transmutation is possible only through

the use of tremendous nuclear energy are no longer defensible. Efforts by the French biologist Louise C. Kervran have shown that spontaneous transmutation is a natural occurrence in organic matter. It now seems evident that the relation between a nucleus and its electrons is different in organic substances than in mineral substances. Some interesting experiments have been carried out with chickens. Hens need calcium to construct the shells of their eggs but in these experiments a number of hens were fed on diets containing no calcium. Their feed was supplemented with mica, a silicate of aluminum and potash. It was discovered that the hens produced the necessary calcium for their egg shells, revealing that potassium together with an ion of hydrogen was transmuted into calcium.

There is a new theory in Russia that is called the Theory of Magic Number which postulates that beyond uranium there are super heavy elements that are stable. It has been the general belief that all elements beyond uranium were radioactive and unstable. So there is current speculation of an element with a weight of 310 and the atomic number of 135. It is being referred to as eka-lead or superlead and small traces of it are said to be naturally present in ordinary lead. An examination of the properties of eka-lead, theoretical at present, reveals that if transmutation were induced, it would likely produce a stable isotope of gold.

As it is now known that essentially atoms are transformed by electric environments, the presence of unusual electromagnetic forces within pyramid space raises the question as to whether transmutation of elements can be occurring therein. The answer at this point in time is not known. What is evident, however, is the phenomena of change—change that is different from that occurring outside the pyramid or in non-pyramidal shaped containers.

When one looks at charts of the electromagnetic spectrum, one learns that the part of the spectrum with waves longer than radiowaves is marked as unknown, as is the other end of the spectrum with waves shorter than cosmic rays. At least part of the force within the pyramid is probably at the short end of the electromagnetic spectrum. This can be assumed as it has been shown that pyramid force will destroy negative bacteria. Tests run for us by a state laboratory revealed that much of the bacteria of contaminated milk was killed in samples placed with pyramids.

In our experiments with meat we discovered that meats will not decay but will rapidly lose moisture and become inert as far as bacteria is concerned. After being in a pyramid for three weeks meat will lose more than 66 percent of its weight but it will not spoil. Compare this with the common use of ultraviolet light to kill harmful bacteria in meat and prevent the formation of other bacteria. Meat can thus be stored at a higher temperature without threat of deterioration.

Wishing to make a comparison test of various edibles, we prepared five identical cardboard pyramids of six-ply posterboard. Each pyramid had a base size of nine and three-eighths inches and stood six inches high. Ventilation was provided for all the pyramids by cutting three-quarter-inch holes from the apex on all sides of the pyramids.

One portion of each food was placed in the King's Chamber area of each of the five pyramids and similar specimens were placed on the table outside the pyramid. We selected four eggs, each weighing 51 grams. Two eggs were left in the shells, one inside and one outside the pyramid, and two eggs were removed from the shells and placed in identical saucers, one inside and one outside. Experiment and control samples were obtained of fresh calf liver, as were two specimens of fish and two samples of sirloin steak. The sirloin steaks were trimmed so that each piece would have what appeared to be the same amount of fat and similar texture. The sirloin steak samples were too large for the small pyramid and were suspended by a nylon cord from the apex of our indoor six-foot pyramid.

All of the foods outside the pyramids each went bad, molded or rotted within the first week. The egg not in the shell was the last to deteriorate by showing mold. None of the food samples inside the pyramids deteriorated; shrinkage and weight loss being the only apparent change. The foods inside the pyramids were weighed as follows:

	Initial Weight	Number of Days in Pyramid	Final Weight
Fresh egg with shell	51 grams	60 days	19 grams
Fresh egg without shell	34 grams	19 days	18 grams
Fresh calf liver	45 grams	20 days	16 grams
Fresh fish	45 grams	15 days	14 grams
Sirloin steak	245 grams	40 days	97 grams

In another test we selected two ripe tomatoes of the same size, each weighing slightly more than seven ounces. One tomato was placed in the King's Chamber area of the six-foot pyramid and the control tomato was placed on a styrofoam block at the side of the pyramid. The tomato outside the pyramid was rotted and had to be discarded by the twelfth day. The tomato inside the pyramid dehydrated but retained its red color and showed no signs of deterioration. The only change noted was the pronounced shriveling of the skin. It was removed after 60 days and when sliced the inside was found to be as firm as when fresh. No deterioration was noted. It weighed slightly more than three ounces.

A large bunch of Concord grapes were divided evenly into thirds. One third was placed at the level of the King's Chamber inside the large pyramid; one third was placed inside a Plexiglass cubicle box outside the pyramid, and the other third was placed on a shelf near the pyramid. Although ventilation was provided for the grapes inside the box, heavy mold developed and nearly filled the box within 10 days. The grapes placed on the shelf started developing mold on the fourteenth day. The grapes inside the pyramid started drying in two weeks time. By the end of five weeks their weight had dropped from the original seven and three-fourths ounces to three and one-fourth ounces. Their minimal weight of two and seven-eighths ounces was reached at the end of seven weeks. They were dry, wrinkled, appearing much like raisins, but had not in any manner deteriorated or developed mold.

In his book, *Supernature,* author Lyall Watson relates that he experimented with pyramids and three items: eggs, rump roast, and dead mice. The control samples were placed in a cardboard shoe box. The ones in the pyramid were preserved and the ones in the shoe box soon smelled and had to be thrown away. He commented, "I am forced to conclude that a cardboard replica of the Cheops pyramid is not just a random arrangement of pieces of paper, but does have special properties."

Dr. Boris Vern, director of the Pyramid Research Project for Mankind Research Unlimited, Inc., Washington, D.C., carried out several experiments with plastic pyramids ten inches high and plastic cubes of equal volume. He reported that raw eggs in the pyramids hardened and dried in less than three weeks. Molds placed on the eggs would not grow. The control eggs remained moist and were receptive to mold growth.

A number of years ago a California researcher, the late Verne Cameron, set a small pyramid in his bathroom, the hottest and wettest room in his house, conditions not very conducive to food preservation. He placed a piece of fatty pork inside the pyramid. After three days he noticed a faint odor but after six more days the smell had vanished and the pork was mummified. The piece of meat remained in the pyramid in the bathroom for several months, and Cameron claimed that it was perfectly edible.

The food preservation aspect, the mummification, and the enhanced dehydration rate, then, gives some indication that the force inside the pyramid is at the short end of the electromagnetic spectrum. But there are magnetic qualities as well, to wit the sharpening effect of razor blades with reports of upwards of 200 shaves from a single blade. The success rate seems to depend on the quality of the blades, those being high-grade steel producing the best results. It would appear that the more non-ferrous material there is in the blade the less effect the pyramid force has on the molecules of the metal. If the force is of the electromagnetic spectrum, as it appears to be, then it would follow that there is a possibility that the force will act in a similar manner to some of the known portions of the spectrum, such as visible light. Visible light is still a puzzle to science; there are theories that appear to answer most of the qualities needed to fit the observable actions of light, but these still remain theory. At present it is assumed that light is an electromagnetic wave, or procession of photons—particles having no mass but possessing energy. Due to this property of light, it is bent or refracted when it passes from one medium to another. For example, when the ray meets a glass surface at an angle, there will be a bending of the ray. Let us assume that the ray penetrates the angled side of the pyramid and in doing so it is bent, perhaps in ratio to the energy particles making up the ray. Assuming that the ray is coming from the west, then the force will travel by reflection inside the pyramid shape, passing periodically by the central point in the pyramid, beneath the apex. This is where all the action is.

The edge of a razor blade has a crystal structure, and crystals grow by reproducing themselves. As the blade becomes blunted, some of the crystals on the edge are rubbed off. Theoretically, the crystals should be able to replace themselves. It is known that sunlight has a field pointing in all directions, and yet sunlight reflected from an object such as the moon is partly polarized and vibrating for the most part in one direction. The edge of a blade could be conceivably destroyed when left in the light of the moon and, actually, this seems to happen. This does not explain, however, the sharpening action of the pyramid. One can only guess that pyramids act as lenses that focus energy, or as resonators that collect energy, thereby encouraging crystal growth.

It is interesting to note that the direction in which a crystal is placed seems to determine the amount of vibratory activity. In his paper, "The Energy Field in Man and Nature," John C. Pierrakos stated that crystals pulsate at different rates, depending on their orientation to the geographic cardinal points. "For instance," he stated, "when the leading edge of a quartz crystal is pointed to the south the pulsatory rate is approximately 9 per minute, when pointed to the west its rate is 6 per minute. It is 4 per minute when pointed north and increases to 14 per minute when pointed east."

To explore this further, it is known that the earth rotates from west to east, and a western stream of force might conceivably, upon contacting the earth's atmosphere, follow it around thus causing the flow of energy to move from the west to the east.

For several years science has known that the air surrounding the earth is slightly ionized. It was at first thought that this ionization was caused by a very penetrating radiation. It was found that the deeper into the ocean that a unit was lowered, the fewer the ionized particles to be found. It appeared that the mass of water absorbed some of the radiation. At first it was believed that the radiations came from radioactivity in the earth itself. But when ion sensing units were sent into the upper atmosphere it was found that the higher the units were sent, the greater the ionization. This indicated that the radiation came from outer space and so the name of "cosmic rays" was given to this force.

The source of this radiation is unknown, except that it comes from somewhere outside the solar system. The force appears to come from all parts of the sky. The distribution of intensities for different latitudes of the earth indicates that the rays are deflected by the earth's magnetic field. Radiation that enters the earth's atmosphere from the cosmos is known as primary radiation, which distinguishes it from radiation that originates inside the atmospheric envelope, such as radiation given off by radium.

Further observations now indicate that this radiation, although coming from all directions, appears to come more from the west than any other direction. The theory is that the rays are caught up in the earth's magnetic field and deflected to the east. This might help explain why our plants inside pyramids move from the west to the east, arch to the south, and repeat the pattern, as described in the chapter, "Pyramids and Plant Power." This also might help explain why razor blades are sharpened inside pyramids only when placed on the north-south axis. This places one edge of a double-edge blade toward the west and the other toward the east. We have found, and others have reported, that on some days a razor blade seems sharper than on other days. Could it be that we are using the edge that has been facing east in the pyramid on one day and possibly the edge facing west on another day?

If water tends to absorb ionized particles, as described above, then the dehydrating effect of the pyramid might also help explain why razor blades stay sharp inside pyramid space.

It is known that water can reduce the firmness of steel by more than 20 percent. The pyramid—or other appropriate resonant cavity—would seem to be the only device that can help the crystal gaps in the razor blade edge by driving out the dipole water molecules by resonant action on the dipole, it has been explained by Karel Drbal, the Czechoslovakian radio engineer who discovered the razor sharpening abilities of pyramids. It can be said, then, that the pyramid dehydrates the edge of the razor blade.

The German scientists Born and Lertes demonstrated that the above action on the dipole-molecules of water is possible in a resonant cavity such as a pyramid when it is fed with appropriate microwave energy. Borns and Lertes found that the microwaves of centimeter-wavelength and their harmonics can produce an accelerated rotation of the water dipole-molecules. This in effect results in a dehydration process, or a driving out of the water dipole-molecules. This would seem to be a process of electromagnetic dehydration.

Why is it then that pyramids constructed of dielectric, or nonconducting material, seem to work better than those constructed of conducting materials? The answer would seem to lie in the fact that microwaves can penetrate the material and feed the resonant cavity of the pyramid.

Pyramids covered with aluminum screen or foil do not seem to exhibit the same qualities as those covered with plastic, wood, canvas, etc. A sheet of aluminum foil or screen placed inside of the pyramid and to the west of a plant inhibits the plant's gyrations; in fact, the plants become totally immobile, according to our time-lapse photography. In the chapter on plants we describe our experiments with metals and plants, but it might be repeated here that aluminum is the only material that seems to present the inhibiting properties. Aluminum is an alloy made by an electrical process and we initially speculated that it acts in a negative or blocking fashion to the energy field entering the pyramid from without. However, we wondered if it might not be providing an additional charge that combined with other electromagnetic forces resulting in an overdose. The fact that magnets placed inside the pyramid also inhibited the gyrations of plants tended to support the latter theory. However, to compound our problem, seeds placed on aluminum foil failed to germinate or germinated slower than seeds placed on other materials. An answer seemed to reside in the evidence that aluminum appeared to hinder enzyme activity. Healers who have been able to improve seed germination and increase plant growth with energy radiating from their hands also are able to increase enzyme activity. A friend of ours, Charles Rhoades, has been quite successful as a healer. Knowing of our experiments with razor blades, he challenged us by proposing to sharpen razor blades by "treating" them with his hands. Some 700 shaves later he is still using the same razor blade with which he started the experiment. Evidently, the qualified healer is able to radiate somewhat the same energy from his hands as that to be found in pyramids. We reasoned that if this energy was somehow blocked by aluminum and inhibited enzyme activity, it would follow that it did the same thing to plants. If this was the case, then a parallel could not be drawn between the effects of aluminum and magnets on plants. Aluminum seemed to serve as a barrier whereas magnets seemed to produce an overdose.

Then we discovered that the apparent blocking action of aluminum was overcome when the material was left inside a pyramid long enough for it to become saturated with pyramid energy. We discovered that aluminum left inside a pyramid for two weeks no longer demonstrated an inhibiting factor to plants. They behaved as though the aluminum were not present. And foil treated in this manner served as a substitute pyramid. The atoms in the aluminum apparently absorbed energy by resonance. When the foil was removed from the pyramid, the atoms were no longer receiving outside energy and the electron orbits started a slow process of decay. As this happened, it released energy and could be used in the same manner as the pyramid itself.

Seeds placed on the treated aluminum germinated as

quickly as those placed inside pyramids, and plants presented similar gyrations as their enclosed peers. We tried an experiment with beef roast. We wrapped two similar pieces from the same roast in treated and untreated aluminum foil. The roast cooked in the treated foil was done in one-third the time required for cooking the roast wrapped in the untreated foil.

In the final analysis, then, we decided that what is apparently happening with the aluminum is that its electrical qualities are such that rather than acting as a blocking mechanism to pyramid energy, as it would at first seem, it absorbs the energy within the pyramid and prevents the energy from otherwise acting on plants, enzymes, etc. Once it is saturated with the energy, it no longer depletes the field and can, then, itself, serve as a resonator of the energy field.

Early in this chapter we mentioned man's affinity for gold and the alchemist's effort to meet the demand for man's most prized possession. The fascination went beyond wealth for in its nature and creation it represented man's most valued states—immortality and spiritual enlightenment. The ancient myths spoke of men of various substances such as iron and silver, and to become the gold man was to reach the highest state and to realize the true purpose of life. Back in the days of pre-history and even to the present day some have believed that certain metals and gems awarded their bearers unusual physical or spiritual gifts. Medicine men of many cultures have worn bracelets and anklets of gold in the faith of their magical qualities. In their original meaning, gold crowns not only represented sovereignty but could endow their owners with strength and wisdom.

Perhaps man's attraction to gold is something buried deep in his unconscious, a long forgotten inherent relationship. We are just beginning to learn from the biochemists the need for small amounts of some metals in our physical bodies. The need for iron and copper is well known and current research indicates that zinc is extremely important to the proper function of the brain. Perhaps we will learn that gold has an even more important role. Edgar Cayce recommended gold in more than forty medical cases. Most of the cases had to do with glandular imbalances.

The need for gold may exist at the cellular level of life for, as described in the chapter on plants, a plant stretched itself almost horizontally in order to wrap itself around gold foil placed near it within a pyramid. However, something must happen to gold foil left in a pyramid for several days. A plant was not attracted to untreated gold foil. The plant continued its usual pattern of movement and growth when untreated gold foil was placed beside it in the pyramids. But when the gold foil was treated inside a pyramid for several days and then placed in a pyramid with the plant, the plant heartily embraced it.

An interesting footnote to the experiment with gold is an experience we had with the movement of a plant. When it was a few inches tall, we placed a young sunflower plant inside a pyramid. It started the west-east movement that we had come to expect of plants. Untreated gold foil was then placed inside the pyramid and when it was removed a short time later, the plant immediately started moving north and south. We do not have an answer as to why the plant would suddenly change directions but we plan to experiment further.

Another experience we have failed to duplicate had to do with brass. We were experimenting with a small strip of thin brass and had placed it on a sharp point in the center of a pyramid. We suddenly noticed that the brass strip was being repelled whenever we brought a hand close to it. Assuming that it was some kind of static charge, we played with it for some time. I (Pettit) thought, "Now my body has perhaps a negative charge and the brass a negative charge," and I wondered if there was any way I could change the polarity of either myself or the strip of brass. And just as I thought this, the strip of brass was drawn to my finger. I continued to play with it and it remained attracted to my finger. But the next morning the brass strip was once again repelled and try as I might I could not change the polarity.

There are reasons for believing that the King's Chamber of the Great Pyramid was specifically designed as a place in which unusual energy fields were generated. The ceiling of the King's Chamber is constructed of nine beams of granite running north and south. Above the King's Chamber there are a total of five chambers, each separated by several feet of air space and alternating layers of nine and then eight granite beams. The final ceiling is composed of huge limestone blocks, which are sloped like a gable roof. The forty-three granite beams are believed to weigh about seventy tons each. The King's Chamber itself is constructed entirely of granite, the floor, all four walls and the ceiling.

Granite is composed of quartz crystals, mica and feldspar and is known to produce a piezo-electric field, particularly when it is under pressure. In this case, the granite is under the pressure of 200 feet of solid limestone above it. The Egyptians referred to granite as "spiritual rock," allegedly because of its electric field. It has been postulated that the Egyptians constructed the King's Chamber in this fashion because the granite under great pressure emitted into the chamber a highly charged field, and that the various layers of granite and air chambers formed a capacitor of permanent charge.

Some scientists have speculated that the Great Pyramid is not only an accumulator of energies but also serves to modify these energies. It has been scientifically shown that any object in which energy vibrates acts as a resonating cavity, and that the energy within the object is focused at a certain point. This applies whether the object is solid or hollow. Therefore, some believe the Great Pyramid may act as a huge resonating cavity able to focus cosmic energy like a giant lens. The highly focused energy would affect the crystals or molecules of any object in the path of the focused beam.

Toth and Nielsen explain that through the use of radiesthesia, or dowsing rods, experimenters have been able to demonstrate that there is a vortex of energy emanating from the apex of the pyramid, which expands in diameter as it rises. Dowsers claimed to have measured a vortex of nearly eight feet in height and with a diameter of six feet above a cardboard pyramid only four inches high. In one experiment, a small pyramid was placed beneath a box and three identical boxes were placed beside it. The dowser, not knowing which box covered the pyramid, tested each box with his rod and the rod reacted only over the box with the pyramid.

The late Verne Cameron invented what he referred to as an aurameter, a device that allegedly measured the force field of persons and objects. He claimed that from a small pyramid he measured a vortex of energy that reached the ceiling. Cameron also claimed that if a pyramid was removed from a spot in which it had stood, it left behind a measurable charge that remained for a number of days.

If a vortex of energy does emanate from the apex of miniature pyramids, we are faced with the question as to the nature of the apex of the Great Pyramid. History does not record any apex on the Great Pyramid nor have signs of one ever been found. Manly Palmer Hall, in *The Secret Teaching of All Ages,* claims that none was intended:

"The size of the capstone of the Great Pyramid cannot be accurately determined, for, while most investigators have assumed that it was once in place, no vestige of it now remains. There is a curious tendency among the builders of great religious edifices to leave their creations unfinished, thereby signifying that God alone is complete. The capstone—if it existed—was itself a miniature pyramid, the apex of which again would be capped by a smaller block of similar shape, and so on ad infinitum. The capstone therefore is the epitome of the entire structure. Thus, the Pyramid may be likened to the universe and the capstone to man. Following the chain of analogy, the mind is the capstone of man, the spirit the capstone of the mind, and God—the epitome of the whole—the capstone of the spirit. As a rough and unfinished block, man is taken from the quarry and by the secret culture of the Mysteries gradually transformed into a trued and perfect pyramidal capstone. The temple is complete only when the initiate himself becomes the living apex through which the divine power is focused into the diverging structure below."

Others are not so sure there wasn't an apex on the Great Pyramid. Cayce stated that the Pyramid was topped with a capstone of unusual crystal that radiated tremendous energy fields. Some believe the capstone was composed of various materials, starting with gold at the lower level and working upward through crystal and finally a diamond or ruby at the very point. George W. Van Tassel, California inventor and director of the College of Universal Wisdom at Yucca Valley, claims that his experiments reveal that a quartz crystal apex on a pyramid model enhances the energy field of the pyramid. He proposed that an apex constructed of laminated quartz, with germanium separating the quartz sheets, would increase the energy fields within a pyramid. There have been speculations that a crystal apex atop the Great Pyramid was used to slow down light rays and thereby extract the magnetic properties of the energy fields. Cayce stated that a person could be rejuvenated by light when it is slowed down.

Whatever the builders of the Great Pyramid gained from its construction may never be entirely known. However, experiments with its small progeny have been sufficiently successful to launch a host of possible future roles for the miniatures. Those not mentioned elsewhere include homes constructed in pyramidal shape; attic air purifiers, raised swimming pools beneath a pyramid canopy, thus creating a large baptismal fount; garbage disposals made feasible by the pyramid's dehydration action on organic materials and the destruction of harmful bacteria; storage for pharmaceutical supplies; sections or even entire supermarkets built in the pyramid shape; pyramid shape living quarters in spacecraft to slow down the metabolic rate of astronauts on long flights; storage units for solar energy; study booths in high schools and colleges; and cells for physical and mental therapy, to name only a few.

The new age of pyramid building may soon be underway.

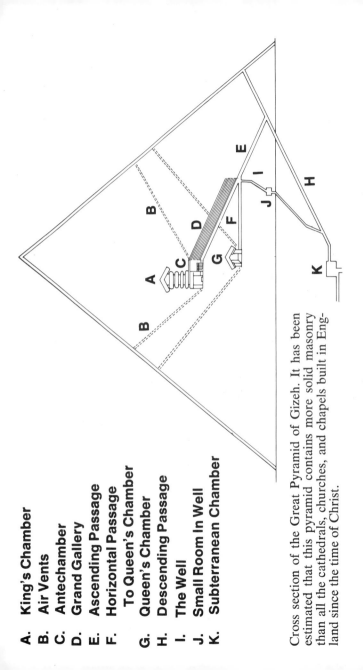

A. King's Chamber
B. Air Vents
C. Antechamber
D. Grand Gallery
E. Ascending Passage
F. Horizontal Passage
   To Queen's Chamber
G. Queen's Chamber
H. Descending Passage
I. The Well
J. Small Room In Well
K. Subterranean Chamber

Cross section of the Great Pyramid of Gizeh. It has been estimated that this pyramid contains more solid masonry than all the cathedrals, churches, and chapels built in England since the time of Christ.

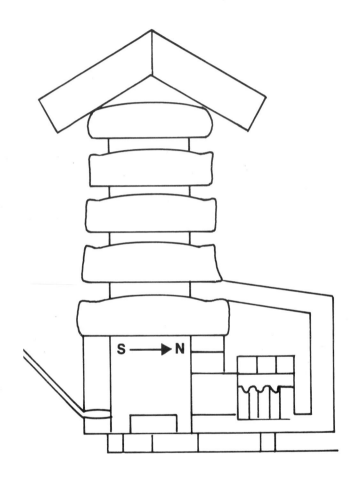

S → N

Detail of King's Chamber. The room is 34 feet long, 17 feet wide, and 19 feet high. The walls, floor, and ceiling are of polished red granite, which may generate electrical qualities.

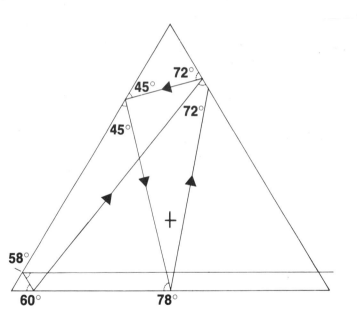

Diagram indicating how a ray of light entering the pyramid at the upper right, for example, is reflected back and forth across the area of the King's Chamber.

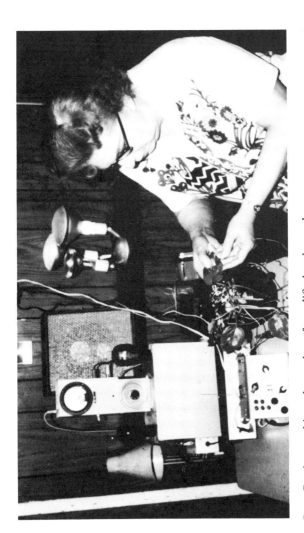

Inez Pettit attaching electrodes of modified polygraph machine to philodendron plant. Effects of placing the plant in a pyramid may then be measured.

Tone experiment with two plexiglass boxes, one inverted over the other, and small PM speaker inside pyramid sounding tones of continuous sustained frequency. Note effect on plant.

Closed-circuit TV monitoring sunflower in pyramid. Note unusual direction of growth.

Sunflower plant inside pyramid. Vertical piece to the rear of the plant is 23K gold leaf. Plant tended to "embrace" the leaf.

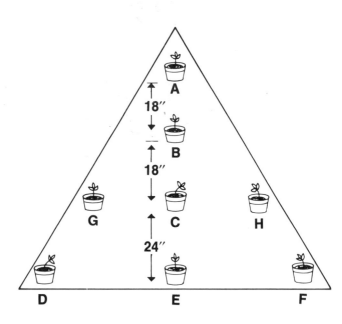

Diagram showing plant location for experiments in growth rates. (See "Pyramids and Plant Power")

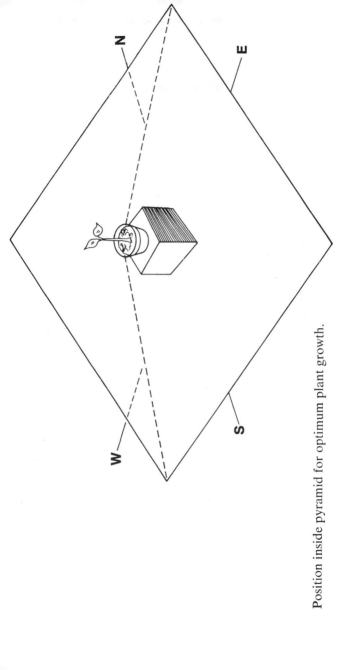

Position inside pyramid for optimum plant growth.

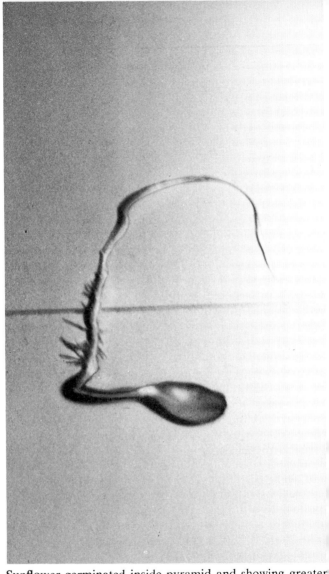

Sunflower germinated inside pyramid and showing greater hairroot development than control plant germinated outside of pyramid.

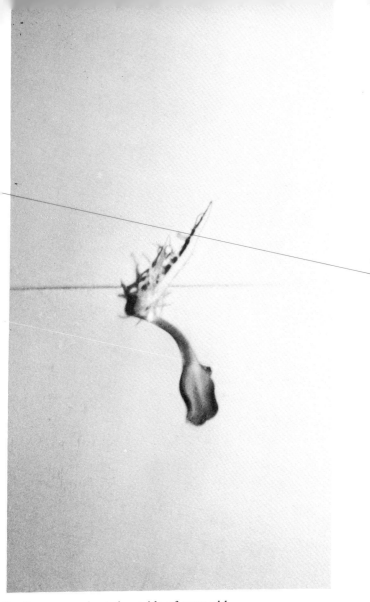

Sunflower germinated outside of pyramid.

Milk sample which has turned to yogurt inside pyramid.

Milk sample which has stratified and is turning to mold (bottom) outside of pyramid.

Sherry Fennell, daughter of Ed Pettit, meditating in outdoor plastic pyramid. People have reported increased sense of awareness and great relaxation from such exercises.

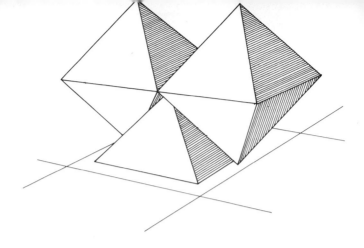

Artist's conception of futuristic pyramid construction. Hospitals, office buildings, and schools might benefit from such construction.

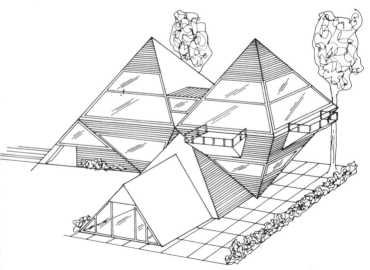

The pyramid house of the future.

7. HEALING POWERS

The tooth had abscessed and was causing considerable pain. Since it was Sunday morning, no dentist was available. Common pain killers had been to no avail. Finally, in desperation, Inez Pettit went inside a wooden pyramid model and sat down, praying for miracles.

What happened she is not sure, but after ten minutes the pain simply faded away. It has not returned to this day. Later inspection by Mrs. Pettit's dentist revealed nothing wrong with the tooth.

We have had a number of people, either using our pyramids or their own, claim relief from a variety of ailments. In cases of sprains, cuts, bruises, strains, infections, etc., healing has apparently occurred in amazing short periods of time.

A friend, Judy Fuller, called one day and said that she was facing dental surgery, was a "bundle of nerves," and wondered if she could sit in one of the pyramids for a while in order to calm herself.

She sat in the pyramid for half and hour and then went directly to the dentist. He injected her gums to deaden the tissue and discovered that the medication wouldn't take. After the fifth injection, he started taking her pulse. He finally resorted to nine injections before obtaining results. The dentist told Judy's husband, Jerry, that he couldn't understand her pulse, that it should be jumping but had shown absolutely no fluctuation. The incision was made, the surgery done on the jaw bone, and sutures taken.

When Judy returned the following day for a checkup, the dentist found her gums a healthy pink and healing definitely in progress. On this occasion and the checkup three days later he simply couldn't understand the fast rate at which healing was taking place.

An understanding of this shortened length of time for the healing process would seem to exist outside the physician's repertoire. But while explanations are absent from medical journals, we find references to this phenomena in the reports on multiwave oscillators or other devices producing electromagnetic waves, and in the literature on spiritual healing. What apparently is occurring is the application of some form of energy that enhances nature's healing process.

Mystics have long claimed that ailments first become manifest within the etheric or electrical envelope of the body and from there are transposed on the physical. This concept has been demonstrated with other life forms. The United States Forestry Department now uses infrared photography to pick up certain types of diseases in trees. It seems that the disease surrounds the trees before it actually enters the material substance of the trees. The infrared reveals the field of the disease before entrance is gained and measures can be taken at an earlier stage. Along this same line of research, those working with Kirlian photography—a high frequency process that photographs the electrical field surrounding plants, animals, and man—have hopes that the process will provide monitoring of diseases at earlier stages of development.

In *The Kirlian Aura,* edited by Dr. Stanley Krippner, it is stated: "An adolescent boy's congenitally defective tibia was stimulated to heal by direct electric current, newly formed bone in the region was produced within two months of electrical treatment. . . . This electric enhancement of bone healing resembles certain types of acupuncture treatment and may provide clues as to the mechanism involved." Also: "There is considerable evidence that both natural and artificial magnetic fields can exert important effects on living organisms."

Our time-lapse films showing plant movement inside pyramids provide evidence that a magnetic field inside a pyramid shape will alter existing forces. Since it is a well-known fact that one magnetic field can disrupt an electron flow, or alter an existing magnetic field, it would seem to follow that we are dealing with some sort of electromagnetic field with the pyramids.

In the chapter on "Pyramids and Plant Power" it was mentioned that the healer Oskar Estebany demonstrated under the supervision of scientist Sister Justa Smith an ability to "generate" a magnetic field equivalent of 13,000 gauss. The energy field generated by Estebany increased seed germination, plant growth, and enzyme activity—the same field, apparently, that makes possible Estebany's successful healing.

An exciting demonstration of the unusual energy generated by skilled healers was conducted in 1974 which is being heralded by science as a breakthrough in producing objective proof of the existence of the healer's power.

Using a laboratory device, a cloud chamber that traces the path of sub-atomic particles through gas, Dr. Robert Miller, professor of chemical engineering at Georgia Institute of Technology for 15 years and now in private industry, and Dr. Philip B. Reinhart, head of the physics department at Agnes Scott College in Atlanta, developed a project to determine if the force exercised by healers could influence the path of the high-energy nuclear particles.

The well-known healer Dr. Olga Worrall, who conducts spiritual healing services in Baltimore, was asked to participate in the experiment, conducted at Agnes Scott College. Prior to Dr. Worrall's involvement, Drs. Miller and Reinhart and a number of others put their hands around the seven-inch chamber. Nothing happened. Then Dr. Worrall placed her hands around the chamber but did not touch it. She concentrated as she does in her healing services and suddenly a dark wave pattern developed in the chamber. "We were looking at energy flowing between her hands. After several minutes, she shifted her position to another point around the chamber. The pattern inside also shifted," Dr. Miller stated. Several professors and graduate students witnessed the experiment and agreed they had seen a true demonstration of the healer's energy manifesting itself.

The two scientists decided to test further. On March 12, from her home in Baltimore, 600 miles from Atlanta, Dr. Worrall concentrated on the cloud chamber and again the unusual pattern appeared. To confirm their findings, the scientists called Dr. Worrall and asked her to repeat her efforts. The result was the same.

"Both times," Dr. Worrall stated, "I could sense the energy flowing out of me. I'm very excited about the results of the test."

Dr. Reinhart commented, "The really amazing thing is when she produced the same effect from 600 miles away. There's absolutely no way she could have done anything to cause that except by mentally transferring her energy."

The Kirlian photographic process has been used by Dr. Thelma Moss at U.C.L.A. to exhibit the energy being radiated from the hands and fingertips of Dr. Worrall. Dr. Worrall showed us a number of the photos taken and it could be clearly seen that there was a considerable difference in the brightness and magnitude of the energy field when she was in a normal state and when concentrating on healing.

We talked with Dr. Worrall about her ability to heal and she told us she has never doubted her abilities but feels that it is important that she demonstrates this force to the satisfaction of science in order for spiritual healing to gain wide acceptance. As Dr. Worrall described some of her cases we were struck once again by the apparent parallels between the case histories of spiritual healing and pyramid healing.

One of the corresponding observations is that water held in a healer's hands was studied under an electron microscope and it was discovered that the hydrogen molecules had moved farther apart . . . the sort of phenomena that would explain the faster evaporation and dehydration produced inside a pyramid.

A year ago I (Pettit) was convinced that I had all the symptoms of prostate trouble and that surgery was just a matter of time. Then I started sleeping in the pyramid two or three nights a week and drinking pyramid water regularly. Six months passed and one day it suddenly came to me that I hadn't experienced any prostate trouble in a long time. A recent checkup revealed that my prostate is completely normal.

In *Pyramid Power* Max Toth and Greg Nielsen state that they have received reports of persons who have felt better even by being near a pyramid model. They state: "Other reports, even more difficult to substantiate, come from people who claim that when they placed a model pyramid near their beds or chairs, after several nights of sleep, or several days of sitting near the pyramid, a specific pain or symptom of illness either disappeared or was greatly alleviated."

If the energy field within the pyramid is greater than that outside and this field tends to produce healthier or healing states, then it can be assumed that the frequencies generated raise the resonant level of cells, tissues, organs, etc., closer to their optimal level of functioning.

"A basic idea in radionics is that each individual organism or material radiates and absorbs energy via a unique wave field which exhibits certain geometrical, frequency and radiation-type characteristics," Dr. W. A. Tiller, head of the Materials Science Department at Stanford University, stated in a paper presented at the Symposium on the Varieties of Healing, sponsored by the American Academy of Parapsychology and Medicine. "This is an extended force field that exists around all forms of matter whether animate or inanimate," Dr. Tiller stated, and continued, "A useful analogy here is the physical atom that is continually radiating electromagnetic energy in the form of waves because of its oscillating electric development and its thermal vibrations. The more complex the materials, the more complex the wave form. . . .

"The fundamental carrier wave is thought to be polarized with a rotating polarization vector. . . . The information concerning the glands, body systems, etc., ripples the carrier wave and seems to be associated with a specific phase modulation of the wave for a specific gland. Regions of space associated with a given phase angle of the wave constitutes a three-dimensional network of points extending throughout space. To be in resonance with any one of these points is to be in resonance with the particular gland of the entity. The capability of scanning the waveform of the gland exists for the detection of any abnormalities. Likewise, if energy having the normal or healthy waveform of the gland is pumped into any of these specific network points, the gland will be driven in the normal or healthy mode. This produces a tendency for its structure to reorganize itself in close alignment with the normal structure, i.e., healing of the gland occurs. Cells born in the presence of this polarizing field tend to grow in a healthier configuration, which weakens the original field of the abnormal or diseased structure and strengthens the field of the normal or healthy structure. Continued treatment eventually molds the healthy organ structure and the condiion is healed.

"All illness has its origin in a disharmony between the mind and spirit levels of the entity and that of the universal pattern for the entity. This disharmony works its way to the physical level via the ratchet effect. Permanent healing and wholeness require that harmony with the universal pattern exist at the mind and spirit levels. Thus, healing at the physical or even the etheric level is only temporary if the basic pattern at the mind and spirit level remains unchanged.

The dependence of life forms on the electrical dimensions is discussed by the eminent astronomer Gustaf Stromberg in *Spiritual Healing*. He states in part: "In order that an organ in our body shall 'become flesh' or become 'incarnated,' certain chemical substances must be present, and they must be assimilated in the immaterial electric finestructure, now known to exist in all living structures. These 'living fields' guide the motions of special types of molecules in such a way that ultimately a complete organ is formed, which itself is an essential part of a living system of a higher order."

The bridge between the chemical and electrical properties of the physical body may reside in the colloidal system. "Colloid" comes from the Greek word for "glue." From atom to molecule to colloid, we are dealing with energy vortexes. A small speck seen under a microscope is many times larger than a colloid, which, like the atom, is not so much a "thing" as it is a unit of energy. The millions upon millions of sensitive colloids holding the body together can be stirred by the smallest vibration. But while colloids are an energy system, when conditions cause them to condense, they pass into a crystaloid state that becomes form. In other words, the energy pattern can be transposed to physical substance, and it well may be that it is at the colloidal level—the stage between vibration and matter—that electromagnetic forces such as those enhanced or generated by the pyramid influence matter.

The use of magnetism to treat the physical body goes back to very ancient times; how far back it is not known but the early Greeks spoke of the use of magnetism in medicine as though the knowledge had been around for a very long time.

The Arabian physician Avicenna used magnets to treat disease of the liver about 1000 A.D., and Ali Abbas, a famous Persian physician in the 10th century, wrote in his *Perfect Book of the Art of Medicine* that magnetism would cure gout and spasms. During the early 1500s the Swiss physician and alchemist Paracelsus used magnets in the treatment of dropsy, jaundice, and a number of diseases. Ambroise Pare in the 16th century reported that some physicians used filings of loadstone and iron to help heal surgical incisions. William Gilbert, Queen Elizabeth's personal physician, disclaimed the effectiveness of magnetism in the art of healing. On the other hand, the American physician Elisha Perkins in 1776 patented Perkin's metallic tractors to cure illness and pain. George Washington was reportedly one of his customers. Later Gaylord Wilshire patented his Ionico, a magnetic collar that allegedly magnetized blood and cured many ailments.

A glance at some of the patents granted in the last hundred years atttests to the continuing role of magnetism as a medical tool. In 1869 a patent was granted for a device which included an elliptical coil for producing magnetic fields in the human body. Shortly thereafter several patents were granted for articles of clothing containing curative magnets.

Dr. E. H. Frei, Benjamin Abrams Professor of Electronics and head of the Weizmann Institute's Department of Electronics, in his article, "Medical Applications of Magnetism," printed in the October 1972 *Bulletin of the*

Atomic Scientists, quotes the description of a patent issued for a magnetic corset:

> The purpose of this invention, the result of long continued experiments and physiological study, is to conveniently apply to the human form magnetic and electric curative appliances, the efficacy of which is now conceded in chest, cardiac, and cerebral affections, especially manifest in persons of nervous temperament and sedentary habits.

Toward the end of the 19th century there were a number of diverse objects patented for medical treatment, including a magnetic chair, hatband, couch, and medallion. In 1904 two patents were granted for machines to treat patients suffering from nervous disorders by producing a magnetic field. A number of other magnetotherapeutic devices were subsequently patented. S. Maeshima of Tokyo received a U.S. patent for an apparatus . . .

> ". . . for transmitting magnetism into the human body, which, giving a slight stimulus to the nerve periphery and tissue cells, accelerates blood circulation and skin excretion and regulates the metabolism, thereby promoting health and keeping off diseases or assisting recovery therefrom."

This patent was issued in 1922, according to Dr. Frei. He also noted that several countries have issued patents for a magnetic shield to protect the hand of the physician from the magnetic field when he applied a small alnico magnet to the heart of his patients.

In 1967 a patent was granted for a machine that produced controllable magnetic fields for medical purposes. It is claimed by this patent that the machine is based on work previously done in the field and also cites work claiming that magnetic fields were able to retard the aging process.

A number of scientific experiments on the influence of magnetic fields were performed in Thomas Edison's laboratory in 1892. Dogs and experimenters themselves were exposed to several thousand gauss without experiencing any ill effects. However, even the weak geomagnetic field, which has a field strength of not more than one gauss, is considered by some scientists to play a role in biological organisms. Some have suggested that birds and sea turtles use the geomagnetic field for navigation and homing, and disturbances of the field in time have been reported to correspond in some way with the statistics of admissions to mental hospitals.

Dr. Frei believes that the equilibrium of chemical processes could be shifted in a magnetic field because of different susceptibilities in the end products. "Any process involving movement of ions could be influenced because of the path of an ion will change in a magnetic field, and this might be an important factor as ions pass through biological membranes," he stated. Mentioned earlier was Sister Justa Smith's work with the influence of magnetic fields on enzyme activity and Dr. Frei notes, "There are indications that the action of enzymes is modified in a field. No rigorous theories exist to explain these magnetic effects although rough analyses show that they should be very small in fields up to several thousand gauss. However, one can assume that in biological systems even very small effects could accumulate and cause significant changes."

Reports from Russia indicate that magnetism has been used in the healing of wounds (Estebany, who was tested by Sister Justa Smith as producing a magnetic field of several thousand gauss, first discovered his healing powers when he found he could treat wounded soldiers) and the growth of tumors, while another work describes that blood-coagulation times may be affected by magnetic fields.

It is known that time-varying magnetic fields produce

electric potentials and known phenomena can be understood in terms of currents derived from such potentials. This includes the so-called magnetic phosphenes. These have been investigated and the effect has been compared to other light-producing stimuli, such as pressure and electric impulses. (The granite slabs around the King's Chamber in the Great Pyramid may produce a piezoelectric effect as a result of the tremendous pressure of the stone above.) Magnetic phosphenes are sometimes said to be tinted light blue shimmering luminosites appearing in the borders of visual fields and are produced by applying 10 to 100 Hz alternating fields to the human head. Some scientists explain this phenomenon by means of electromagnetic induction as a result of the changing magnetic fields. Still this theory does not take into account the underlying phenomenon and does not explain how the light is physically produced. While most researchers contend that the effect is only seen in the light, other evidence would indicate that it has also been observed as occurring in darkness. Staring at a specific object increases the effect.

It is interesting to note that one of the metaphysical exercises for the ability to read auras is the development of peripheral vision. This electrical envelope around both animate and inanimate objects, but particularly humans, is sometimes seen as a thin blue light. Dr. Pierrakos, whose work is described elsewhere in this book, developed a type of blue glass in order to better see the aura or etheric field around plants, animals, and humans. Following this line of thought, reports that sometimes the Great Pyramid radiates a pale blue light would support theories of its magnetic qualities.

While testing some of the concepts developed by Baron Reichenbach concerning the nature of Odic force, Prof. D. Enlicher of Vienna observed that electromagnetic flames sometimes reach 40 inches and exhibit a rich play of colors ending in a luminous smoke of pale blue color.

Along these lines some attention should be given to the bibliography appearing in the second quarter issue of the *Electronic Medical Digest,* in 1959, under the title "Does Alternating Low Frequency Magnetic Energy Affect Living Tissue?" This bibliography covers some of the scientific experiments conducted in an effort to find the answer to this question. According to a two-year study carried out at the American Institute of Radiation at Belmont, California, the answer would be yes. The bibliography lists 27 writers, with references to numerous technical magazines. The articles are not confined to the effect of alternating low-frequency fields, but in many instances are concerned with the therapeutic effects of permanent magnets, on tissues, cellular growth, relief of pain and of nervous conditions, tumors, growth reactions in plants, etc. A great deal of relevant material is to be noted in the development of radiesthesis, particularly in Europe, in the expanding studies of the nature of the aura and the etheric body and in the whole field of medical electronics.

The appearance of the blue color is sometimes mentioned by persons who have sat or meditated in pyramids. Wilhelm Reich claimed that the color of orgone energy, the mass-free cosmic life energy, was blue. The orgone energy accumulator is a six-sided box known as an "oraccu." The sides are made of alternating layers of organic and inorganic materials. The inner wall is lined with a thin sheet of sheet iron. This arrangement allegedly makes possible a concentration of atmospheric orgone energy much greater than normal.

Subjects tested after a short period of time in oraccus produce blood samples revealing orgonotic charge of red blood cells. "The charge reveals itself, after autoclavation, in the blue bions," Wilhelm Reich stated in *The Cancer Biopathy.* He added, "The lack of orgonotic charge manifests itself, after autoclavation, in the absence of the blue bions and in the presence of T-bacilli, which result from the degeneration of the red corpuscles (T-reaction).

"The T-reaction is typical for cases of advanced cancer in which the orgone content of the blood has been totally consumed in the organism's struggle against the systematic disease (cancer biopathy) and the local tumor. This T-reaction is usually present before any symptoms of anemia and often reveals the cancer process long before a perceptible tumor has formed. . . . On the other hand, red corpuscles weak in orgone energy absorb it greedily when it is supplied to the organism by the orgone accumulator. Subsequent autoclavation tests yield a shift from the T-reaction to the B-reaction, i.e., the red blood corpuscles have become more resistant to autoclavation; they contain more orgone. . . . The red corpuscle can be charged by atmospheric orgone energy."

Dinshah P. Ghadiali, an Indian scientist greatly influenced by the research of Dr. Jagadis Bose, whose work is discussed in the chapter on plants, founded a system of treatment by the use of colored lights, which he called "Spectro-Chrome Metry." According to Ghadiali, blue light radiation soothes inflammations, does away with infections, and brings about healing through balancing the electrochemical properites of the body.

Blue light neutralizes the hydrogen of red, according to Dinshah Ghadiali, and "As the affinity of hydrogen, this attuned color wave represents the oxygen. Water, H_2O is the outcome of the chemical combination of hydrogen and oxygen and is another proof of the mathematical precision with which spectrochrome is built. It is the most neutral compound. . . . The diaphoretic effect is the result of the hydrogen in febrile and inflammatory processes being conquered by the oxygen. Hence, in reality the refrigerant or cooling effect of the blue depends upon the production of the perspiration, because, under a law of chemistry, evaporation always evolves cold owing to an expansion in the composing molecules, parting with heat," he states in Volume 3 of his *Spectro-Chrome Metry Encyclopedia.*

More light on the phenomena is shed by Reich in *The Cancer Biopathy:* "The red corpuscle is an orgonotic system in miniature, containing a small quantity of orgone energy inside its membranes. At 4000x magnification, the red blood corpuscles show a deep blue glimmer and lively vibration of their contents. They expand and contract and are therefore not rigid, as is usually thought. They carry atmospheric orgone energy from the lungs to the tissues. The nature of the relationship between atmospheric oxygen and orgone energy can only be surmised at this time. Whether orgone is identical with the chemical particles of the air or fundamentally different from them is unknown. . . . The orgonotic charge is also revealed in the shape and structure of the red blood corpuscles. Cells with a weak charge are more or less shrunken and have a narrow blue margin which glimmers feebly. Once the organism is charged, the red blood cells swell, while the blue margin intensifies and widens, sometimes including the entire cell. No pathogenic microorganism can survive in the vicinity of these orgonotically highly charged red blood cells."

The research of Reich and Ghadiali would indicate that some kind of energy field exists in the atmosphere that can be accumulated and directed toward the electrochemical properties of the physical body in beneficial ways. References to the blue light or auras would seem to point to the presence of electromagnetic qualities in the energy field being generated. Observations of blue light around pyramids or reported by persons sitting or meditating within pyramids provide some evidence that the pyramid shares in the phenomena of producing identical or similar electromagnetic forces. These observations, along with the similarities between the descriptions of treatment of diseases and afflictions by blue light, orgone energy, and various forms of electromagnetic therapy and those reportedly produced by the pyramid, would seem to point to common denominators.

In any case, our experiments and those of others revealed every indication of some healing phenomena occurring as the result of pyramid power. We have repeatedly healed cuts, bruises, sprains, etc., in less than the expected time, and following are a few statements by individuals representative of the many we have received in regard to healing experiments:

Florence Hill: "Several teeth were aching and after a while in the pyramid my teeth stopped aching but I could still feel a force going to my teeth. I felt a tingling sensation all over my extremities. I think my heart slowed down and I seemed to see a lot of blue color."

Effie Jorgensen, experience in pyramid meditation tent: "Went in with sinus congestion, aching throughout body. In for one hour and head felt much better. I had a buzzing sensation while I was in for the first 30 minutes. Sinus drainage was good; after one hour joints were not aching."

Mary Stoldt: "My husband had a chronic backache and got relief." And on another occasion: "Extremely bad headache. Sat for only 20 minutes and head improved."

Dave Wilcox: "I have a large pyramid in my bedroom under which I sleep. My energy level is higher than before and I feel healthier than I ever have."

J. M.: "I had had an accident and sitting in the pyramid has helped me gain great mobility of my limbs."

One woman had a wartlike growth on her thumb for eleven years and the more she picked at it the larger it became. She placed the thumb under a small pyramid for two 15-minute periods on the same day and the wart was gone on the following day.

A man told us that he had been suffering from poison-ivy infection for a number of days but that the infection completely cleared the day following treatment by sitting in a pyramid. Another man reported that after working with pyramids for a time that his pulse dropped from the 80s to the 60s.

We placed a gerbel inside a small pyramid. As long as she lived inside the pyramid structure, her housekeeping was neat and her nest orderly. When her cage was moved outside the pyramid, she scattered litter everywhere. On one occasion she cut her face badly on the cage and we even thought she would lose one of her eyes. No medication was used on either the cut or the eye, but after being placed beneath the pyramid once more her eye completely healed, the scar disappeared, and the fur grew back as normal.

As regards the medical use of electromagnetic fields, Dr. Frei in the article mentioned earlier states that muscle stimulation is an area where some research has recently been conducted and that results show that practically all muscles will contract as the magnetic field on them is altered. "It is widely assumed that the stimulation is of an electrical nature caused by electromagnetic induction," he states. "An electric field produced by a changing magnetic field can send a current through a cell and in this way stimulate all kinds of muscles. . . . The importance of muscle study lies in the possibility of stimulating the heart muscle which could be of prime importance in emergency pacemaking before electrodes can be inserted internally."

In other areas of medical application Frei points out: "A further application of such stimulation might lie in the possible stimulation of the cortex. There is hope that by employing properly designed time varying magnetic fields one could stimulate phenomena in the brain which otherwise can only be produced by inserting electrodes below the skull."

A well known and highly successful chiropractor told us that he charged a small metal plate by placing it on top of a series of miniature pyramids. The metal pyramids are joined at their bases in a rectangular shape, five units by three units, fifteen in all. He uses the charged plate in order to raise the biorhythm of afflicted parts of the body and claims that it is quite successful.

According to an article several years ago in *Fate* magazine by Joseph F. Goodavage, a New York City gynecologist and cytologist, Dr. K. E. MacLean, used an electromagnetic activator in the treatment of advanced cases of cancer. Goodavage quoted MacLean as saying, "Cancer cannot exist in a strong magnetic field."

According to Goodavage, a side effect of the treatment was the restoration of pigmentation in the hair, "in most cases from a silvery white to its former natural color. Dr. MacLean's full head of hair is dark brown; he has been exposing himself to a 3600 gauss magnetic field daily for about five years. He is tall and athletic-appearing and looks to be about 45 years old. He is 64."

The particular shape of the pyramid aligned on the north-south axis is what produces the unusual energy field, according to what we've learned from our experiments. While the traditional pyramid shape may not be the only one that generates or enhances energy fields—as we discovered in testing the cone shape on plants—our investigations revealed that cubes do not produce the same results.

Yet we spend most of our lives inside cube-shaped structures. Unwisely, according to Buckminster Fuller, scientist, mathematician, author, architect, and inventor of the geodesic dome. Fuller believes that homes, office buildings, churches, or any type of building for that matter, should be other than cube shape, and explains that this is particularly true of hospitals or other places of healing.

Perhaps the "cubes" in which we live distort or somehow inhibit energy fields in such a manner that we are either cut off from their beneficial influence or are negatively bombarded by altered wave forms. It well might be that preventive medicine of the future will be practiced by the engineers and architects. Homes may then be promoted for their therapeutic qualities.

8. REJUVENATION

Today it is vitamin E, zinc tablets, and rose hips that are being bantered as balms for staying young, but today's tonic may be tomorrow's old wives' tale. Still the search goes on, in the latest formula of cucumber oil or peach soap it goes on, through Formula X, face lifts, salt spring baths, the latest isometrics, dosages of panthothenic acid and bee pollen, and yoga breathing, it goes on.

All the approaches are not equal, of course, and some of the above undoubtedly have their merits. Certainly, some strong cases can be built around the youth-giving qualities of vitamins and few will argue the value of correct breathing and proper exercise. Yet, man is not entirely satisfied with these results; somehow he thinks he can do better.

Some believe there are precedents for extending our three-score and ten upon this earth. They point to Old Testament personages who allegedly lived several hundred years, and the legends surrounding Atlantis where the residents did equally well. For those seeking more current material, references are made to certain holy men of India and Tibet who reportedly push their time well into the second century or even beyond.

Several years ago, our teacher, Swami H. H. Rama, a highly trained Indian scientist, told us that his guru was nearly 150 years old and that this could be proven. When we asked him how he was able to live that long, we were told, "Because he has learned to use certain energy fields for that purpose." We have no reason to dispute his word, particularly since such stories are not uncommon. A friend of ours spent some time in the Himalayas and claimed to have had contact with several holy men, living in seclusion, whose memories stretched far back into the nineteenth century.

Jack Parr, an Englishman, lived to be 175 years old. He became quite a celebrity and died, apparently, of overindulgence during a party thrown for him at the royal court. An autopsy revealed that there was nothing particularly wrong with him beyond an excess of wine, food, and song.

And magazines and newspapers of late have carried a number of articles on Russia's centurians, some still working at 130 and 140 years of age. So . . . our elder citizens may not necessarily be dreaming the impossible dream. Perhaps some secrets are hiding out there somewhere. But where? Ah, that's the rub. But well-credited and intended scientists are now trying to isolate the important components of perpetuating youth. The more visible factors—diet, environment, life-styles—are believed to play contributory roles. Probing deeper, however, there seems to be a general concensus that the retention of health and youth must be examined at the cellular level, where all the action takes place. Within this focus, questions are being asked as to why cells deteriorate and die, and why the difference in the rate of cell birth versus cell death.

According to more than a few leading scientists, the newest and most promising field of medicine is bioelectrics, the study of the electromagnetic nature of the body. Bioelectrical approaches do not deny the importance of mechanical and chemical factors in the maintenance of the physical body. However, they do contend that to overlook the role played by electromagnetic or other energy fields is to settle for a partial and distorted view.

The energy field of the body apparently is not entirely limited to the physical structure but radiates through and somewhat beyond these confines. This energy field appears to be the same as that referred to by mystics and clairvoyants as the aura, and, according to them, deterioration of cells, tissues, organs, etc., occur first within the aura. It can then become manifest within the physical body, or it can possibly be cured or controlled at the bioelectrical level.

One energy field theory contends that all cells capable of reproduction contain in their nuclei filaments of highly conductive material surrounded by insulating media. This filament, which some believe to be the DNA-RNA complex, is always in the form of a spiral or helix; in other words, a coil. Therefore, each cell and its filament may react as a tuned circuit if its resonant frequency can be approximated by an external oscillating source. It has been proposed by Lakhovsky, developer of the multiwave oscillator, and by others that by exciting the nuclei with electromagnetic energy a change can be induced by the long established principle of electromagnetic induction. This allegedly raises the energy level and perhaps the vitality of every cell simultaneously.

Now, the interesting thing is that, according to research to date with pyramids, there are some indications that these electromagnetic fields, and additional unnamed energy fields, described as being used in various kinds of electrotherapy, are likewise being produced in pyramid structures. It may be that electromotive forces produced or enhanced by the pyramid shape can raise the cell's metabolic rate by electrolysis, and perhaps jog the DNA-RNA "memory" and reproductive capabilities to their level at an earlier, younger age, thus rejuvenation.

One of the uncovered factors seemingly contributing to the longevity of Russia's centurians is the use of electromagnetic therapy. We have heard little about this particular component in this country for it is suspect in most medical circles. But in parts of Europe and Asia where a new look is being taken of the works of Mesmer, Reich, Reichenbach, et al, bioelectrical medicine is being pioneered within the framework of the new technologies. Scientists investigating these fields of endeavor are coming back to tell us that we should wake up to a whole "new" field of exciting exploration with proven results.

Aaron H. Steinberg, Ph.D., undertook such a mission and wrote a thought-provoking article, "Upgrading Cellular Activity With Electromagnetism," for the *Journal of Borderland Research*.

"For too many years now the scientific knowledge of electromagnetics and its positive effects on cell life has been collecting dust and cobwebs on the shelves of ignorance, brought on by those special interests who fear the Truth. We are now seeing a rebirth, if you will, with scientists both professional and amateur, who are reviewing the work of their predecessors and making improvements in the mechanical application of magnetic fields," Steinberg writes.

He went to Russia in 1969 to gain a firsthand look at the work being done there with electromagnetism. "In several country homes for retirees," he said, "I was most pleasantly surprised to see electromagnetism used daily on most of the old folks. I should say young folks since many who claimed to be over 100 years young, looked and acted like most people at 50! The main object of the

E-M (electromagnetism) was to reverse the aging process by altering the cellular structure. I was most anxious to purchase a piece of equipment, but alas no sale.

"Seek and you shall find has always been one of my dominant characteristics. So when I learned that Japan was truly advanced in this field, having been using such equipment since 1936, I decided to go there in 1970. I sought out the one company that had been most productive in this field. They were most kind and cooperative. I was introduced to several scientists who had done much useful research. Their claims were backed up by scientific facts and I was convinced that they had a well constructed instrument, simple to use by anyone so desirous. They named their equipment The Magnetizer."

Steinberg purchased a magnetizer and brought it back to the United States where he immediately initiated research with the device. "I can report that the results obtained to date have been most favorable," he states, "after nine months of experimentation. The magnetic flux generated by the coils can be measured accurately over any part of the body, thus determining those areas where the flux is penetrating as well as those where it is weak.

"Chemicals and pollution are surely contributing to an unhealthy alteration in our cellular activity and human magnetic field. It will be many years, if at all, before this mess can be rectified and controlled. But in the meantime, those who are aware and see the danger signals, will not sit by and wait for the clean up, which may never happen. Instead they will seek to upgrade their cellular activity so that the body's natural resistance may be at peak ohms. There is some indication that the aura force centers known as chakras or vortexes are stimulated by electromagnetism."

According to Steinberg, he spent some time discussing theory with the Japanese scientists and learned that the magnetic flux is different from ordinary electric current, which only flows along the surface of physical matter. It is also different from X-rays that do not penetrate the bones. On the other hand, the magnetic flux of ultra-long waves generated by the magnetizer penetrates deeply in muscles, fat, and bones and has an intensive effect on the nerves.

"Magnetic flux never causes unpleasant sensations on the body, such as pain or shock, but instead produces comfortable warm sensations," Steinberg claims. "These sensations are also known as Joule's heat, which strengthens the function of the cell, corrects spasms and inflammations. When magnetic flux passes through tissues, a secondary electric current called the eddy current is created around the magnetic lines of force in the tissue cells, which ionizes the protoplasm and rejuvenates the tissues as a result of activating metabolism. Furthermore, magnetic flux, in the process of penetrating the tissues, works to increase hormone secretions. These maintain youth by providing energy as a result of normalizing function of the internal organs. . . . Flux strongly stimulates magnetic substances in the blood, like iron. Accordingly, the hemoglobin in the blood vessels moves actively, accompanying the lymph circulation, when the Magnetizer is turned on. The therapeutic effect is not singular but collective, thus eliminating constitutional weakness."

Researchers in the field contend that electromagnetic forces "must" influence the tissue rate of vibration. Drs. Abrams and Drown postulated that tissues and organs when vibrating at their optimum rate were healthy. If the vibratory rate decreased, then disease occurred. Abrams and Drown believed that if one could "beam in" with the correct rate of electromagnetic vibration, the diseased tissue or organs would use the force to increase its rate of vibration and regeneration could take place. Some scientists today, however, believe that Abrams and Drown were too narrow with their concept inasmuch as with their model it was necessary to learn the individual's rate of vibration, or an organ's rate of vibration, before treatment could take place. On the other hand, if a wide spectrum of vibrations is used, such as with the multiwave oscillator, then one of the waves being produced will correspond to that of the tissue or organ and treatment can ensue. That is the theory, anyway, and a growing number of case studies would indicate confirmation.

Considerable research will be necessary before any conclusion can be reached as to the value of the pyramid in the field of bioelectrics. We would not wish to indicate otherwise. Nevertheless, the superficial and informal exploration of pyramid forces to date give us some reason to believe that we are dealing with a structure producing energy fields similar or identical to those produced by other electromagnetic devices; the nondeterioration of organic materials; the youthful appearance of skin treated with pyramid water; the healing properties, the unusual subjective states of awareness, etc. Our hypothesis is that the more we learn about energy fields, the more we will understand pyramids, and the greater our understanding of the forces at work within the pyramid, the more we can contribute to energy field theories.

More than 50 years ago an English scientist, A. E. Baines, stated in a paper entitled "The Origin and Problem of Life" that there are at least three things that militate against a continuance of vigorous life for prolonged periods. One is physical deterioration; another is gradual failure of generation of nerve force; and the third a falling off in the production of certain glands that vitalize body and brain.

"We have then, to deal with deficiencies, deficient nerve force and, it may be, deficient insulation, the latter with special regard to the effective functioning of certain glands, which may receive a normal supply of energy but by reason of defective insulation fail to retain or fully utilize it," Baines stated, and continued, "Nor is that all. The impulses which stimulate and activate our glands pass from the brain through the secretory and if they are not retained or utilized fresh demands are made upon the brain to replace the wastage.

"First of all, we require a means of generating nerve force in order to be able to supply it. For years we have heard of a new force called Odic and Psychic by Sergeant Fox and Sir William Crooks, respectively. It has been associated in the minds of most people with the occult, probably because no one has yet been able to demonstrate satisfactorily its nature, its value to humanity, or even to evolve it. The ancient Egyptians could, there is reason to believe, do so and, but for the burning of the library in Alexandria, might have been disclosed before the Christian era. My knowledge of the new force, which I have called Vitic, came about in a curious way. Years of residence in Egypt had created an interest in Egyptology, an interest which, upon my returning to England, drew me not infrequently to the galleries of the British Museum.

"In the bygone days of Egypt's greatness, scientific attainment was confined to the priestly communities, and they kept it from the outer and unlearned world under the veil of an elaborate symbolism. Even then it appears likely that the search for the Elixir of Life had begun. When, therefore, I noticed that a statue of one of the priests was shown holding a cylinder in one hand, my curiosity was aroused and I determined upon an investigation. That the reigning Pharoah was similarly equipped merely suggested reasonable concession on the part of the priesthood, and in no way negated the supposition that the cylinders or short rods had some purpose or function of an important nature of which they were symbolical in the statutory.

"The most prominent statue, a painted limestone portrait, dates back to about 3700 B.C., and is a royal personage named An-Kheft-Ka, who is shown holding a rod in each hand, much in the manner that a runner holds corks. In my belief, as I have said, these rods were symbolical; but of what? Surely not of power; for that on the part of priestly communities would have been to court disaster at the hands of a jealous and incensed Pharoah. What was the keynote of ancient Egyptian character? Sensuality, perhaps; virility in greater probability; for sensuality would not so freely advertise itself. That was the conclusion to which I finally came. Diligent inquiry of the authorities at the Museum elicited the astonishing fact that nothing was known of the purpose or meaning of the rods. They had no information whatever.

"Years of experiment followed in the effort to discover something which when held in the hand would beneficially affect the nervous system. Finally it was found, by accident, in carbon. Hard carbon such as is used in arc lamps will give out a certain amount of force which, experience has taught us, is not to be distinguished from nerve force. But if the carbon is treated in such a manner as to cause a violent disturbance of its molecules and then specially hardened, the force evolved by it is greatly augmented, and the rod becomes a real source of power, a power that is so readily absorbed and stored by the unipolar ganglion cells that a five-minutes' charge remains effective for at least twelve hours."

Writing of Baines's hypothesis that an electric wave is not simple but compound, Dr. White Robertson stated in his book, *Electro-Pathology*, published in 1918: "That the second alternative is not far-fetched is suggested by a recent discovery of Baines, that by a special hardening process applied to ordinary arc-carbon, a 'new force' has been found to reside in the altered carbon which can be conveyed to and stored in the body for a period of several hours by simply holding these in the hand, with the result that subnormal galvanometric deflections are enormously enhanced; and already we have been able to observe gratifying changes in cases of nervous breakdown apparently by increasing the nerve charge through these carbons. What this force is we do not as yet know, nor is it known to the eminent physicists and physiologists to whom we have demonstrated it. It is not magnetic. And if it differs from an electric charge in that it is not readily diffused, but is, as registered by the galvanometer over a period of twelve hours, stored probably in the unipolar ganglia of the nervous system."

In an article published in *The Practitioner*, June 1914, Dr. J. Horne Wilson wrote of Baines's discovery "In this connection (nerve deafness), I may mention that a rod of carbon, which has its molecular condition altered in a similar way to that of iron when it is converted into a magnet, has a most remarkable effect on the body deflections. If held in the right hand, it produces an off-scale positive deflection (on the galvanometer), and an off-scale negative if held in the left hand. If held in contact with the right side of the body for five or ten minutes, it makes the hand-to-hand deflections strongly positive, and has exactly the opposite effect if held on the left side of the body. What this force is I do not at present pretend to say, but it has a marked influence on the electrical conditions of the body, though no direct influence upon the terminals of the galvanometer. It evidently charges the body with a force akin to nerve energy, as it is retained for a much longer period than electricity is."

And Wilson wrote in the July 25, 1914 issue of *The Medical Times:* "This form of energy will raise the nerve currents to normal. The rod held in the right hand acts as a stimulant without any depressing after-effect, and in the left hand a sedative. Under its stimulating influence the nervous system is generally benefited; mental fatigue rapidly disappears, and morbid conditions such as neurasthenia, insomnia, and feeble action of the heart readily yield to it.

"The second cylinder shown in the left hand of An-Kheft-Ka was probably of minor importance and was not of the nature of carbon, as that would have neutralized the charge. It was, I have little doubt, fashioned from a piece of magnetic iron ore. Magnetism applied to the left side of the body stimulates the heart action, but only so long as the body remains within the magnetic field. The properties of magnetic iron ore—and perhaps these properties—were known to the Chinese in olden times, and also to the earlier Greeks who, as likely as not, gained their knowledge from the Egyptians.

"If two rods are held, the carbon in the right hand and the permanent magnet in the left, the effect is accentuated; but while the charge imparted by the carbon endures for some twelve hours, that exerted by the magnet ceases to be operative upon relinquishment."

The account by A. E. Baines leaves much to be desired. It would help if we had some knowledge of what his "years of experiment" were more specifically devoted to, and by what "accident" the force was found in carbon, and how it was that he determined that arc-carbon gives out "a certain amount of force not to be distinguished from nerve force." It would also help to know what the preliminary treatment of carbon should be, and what is meant by the "special hardening" process. We are offered no insights as to how he knows that this force is then greatly augmented and that it is stored by the unipolar ganglion cells. It would seem that Dr. Robertson accepted the statements as factual, although he provides no further information. He did offer, however, several conclusions gleaned from his own research. The information provided by Dr. Wilson in his two articles apparently is provided from his own study and research.

The objective evidence seems to be limited to readings on the galvanometer. A number of reports of beneficial results from having used the rods have been collected over the years by the Borderland Sciences Research Foundation. Yet, we cannot overlook the possibility that suggestion may play an important part. Efforts have been made with most of the experiments to reduce or even eliminate suggestion as having an influence, but common sense tells us that definite conclusions cannot be drawn. It would seem necessary to seek further verification that both normal and subnormal galvanometric deflections are increased by use of the carbon rods. Also, there is a need to determine whether the effects are forthcoming only from the carbon or whether similar results can be obtained from using rods made of other metals, and with and without the magnet. Further, there is a need to verify the claim that the force or energy can be stored in the body for several hours after the rods are used.

If these experiments are verified and it is determined that some energy field does enter and is stored in the human body using the rods, we will still need to demonstrate the connection, based primarily on the similarity between the results obtained in both areas of investigation. One of these interesting parallels concerns the variation in results obtained by different individuals. Whether using the carbon rod or the pyramid, most subjects have reported beneficial results. A few have claimed the carbon rod overstimulates them even to the extent that they cannot sleep. And a small number of subjects have claimed they can stay in the pyramids for a very short time without getting headaches or feeling in some manner upset. In both cases, the "charge" is apparently too much for them.

On the other hand, quite a large number of people have told us that they feel vitalized and "more alive" after spending some time inside a pyramid. Not only are their perceptions sharpened but senations seem enlivened.

One interesting story was told us by a man's wife. In his early fifties, he built a pyramid after hearing one of our lectures and started treating water in it. He used the water on his house plants but also started drinking it regularly. A few weeks later, his wife said to us, "I think I'm going to have to cut Henry's water off or start drinking it with him." When we queried her, she confessed,

"Well, I think he must be regressing to his twenties or thirties. He hasn't been this sexually aroused for years!"

Al Manning, director of E.S.P. Laboratory, Los Angeles, relates that author David Sinclair spent several minutes in a pyramid and had to step out as he became dizzy. The strange feeling remained with him after he returned home. He canceled out on a party and instead took a nap. Yet, when he awakened three hours later, according to Manning, Sinclair felt like he had slept for days.

It should be remembered that, according to our experiments with germination and plant growth, the energy field within a pyramid was not always the same. In the carbon rod experiments, the magnet allegedly is the acting force upon the cells of the body and attracts the carbon. Magnets placed near plants have reportedly increased their growth, while magnets placed inside pyramids seem to retard growth—again, an apparent matter of too great a charge, or perhaps, a negation of one energy field by another.

Another source that credits the ancient Egyptians with a knowledge of energy fields and their effects on rejuvenation of the human body is the strange journal of Count Stefan Colonna Walewski, *A System of Caucasian Yoga*. This was the first and probably the only edition of the Count's journal and it was published by the Falcon's Wing Press in 1955.

The editor's preface to the journal states: "Count Stefan Colonna Walewski's outer life was that of a well-known collector and dealer in oriental art and antiquities and in anthropological curios. His shop, Esoterica, was not only a famous New York connoisseur's landmark but the gateway of another world, in which magic, demons and talismans were as real as subways and neon signs. The Count firmly believed that he attracted these strange objects to him by a sort of higher magnetism of which he knew the workings; and his unrivaled collection seemed to prove his point.

"Few knew, however, that behind Count Walewski's constant kindnesses to his fellow man and his expert knowledge—the two main faces of his external life—there lay an intense inner life and search for life's hidden secrets. Few knew that before the 1920s, in the Caucasus mountains (between the Black and Caspian seas, on the border between Turkey and Russia) he had been vouchsafed some of those secrets by two initiates of a rarely encountered secret society, which combined indigenous doctrines and those of yoga with teachings stemming from a mystical tradition of ancient Zoroastrianism. Walewski never saw his teachers again, and he himself assumed no personal credit for their teachings, which were merely handed on to him under oath not to reveal the source. Their instructions, received in Persian and Russian, were transcribed in a manuscript notebook from his own notebook, by the Count, when he later arrived in America, coming first with a Polish diplomatic commission. The English of the transcription is halting and the orthography often incorrect as Count Walewski possessed but an imperfect knowledge of English at that time."

In this journal is found the following: "IX L Arcane. Recharging nervous energy. A way used in ancient Egypt for strengthening of currents of energy within the body. It was shown in the figures, using the second Master Arcane exercise. Two rods clasped in the hands of standing figures, were the grips of tremendous power, akin to electricity (secondary electricity), which when the grips were held in the hand released this energy into the body, to be stored in unipolar ganglias, and spinal fluid, raising the potential of energy 100%, and lasting for a day and a night, 24 hours."

Again, the importance of this information to pyramid research seems to rest with the question as to what extent the ancient Egyptians understood the nature of energy fields. If they knew how to produce and make use of these forces, then it is not unreasonable to assume that in their greatest accomplishment—the Great Pyramid—they made use of this knowledge.

9. THE VOICE OF THE PYRAMID

Sir W. Siemens, a British inventor, stood in amazement atop the Great Pyramid of Gizeh, watching sparks issue from the raised fingers of his Arab guide. He claimed the phenomena produced a distinct ringing sound. Over 200 years ago, Nathaniel Davidson, the British consul-general in Algeria, stood in the Grand Gallery of the Great Pyramid and noted the strange resonance in echoes reverberating from his voice.

The presence of sound apparently is not limited to the great stone pyramid. A number of individuals have told us they heard unusual sounds while inside pyramid models. The reports vary as the experiences affect persons differently, but most mentioned a "kind of distant ringing" or "echoing." The sound seemed to correspond to impressions of "tingling" or "vibrations from within." We discovered that other pyramid experimenters had similar experiences.

Evidence that the pyramid shape acts as a sound resonator and apparently produces beneficial vibrations can be drawn from the parallel effects from experiments with sound and with pyramid replicas. Musical tones have been used to seemingly affect healing, change material substances, and influence plant growth, and subjects and objects subjected to pyramid power experience similar metamorphoses. Apparently sound waves are a form of energy and energy affects cells.

Sound was thought to be the principle tool of healing by the ancients, including the Egyptians, who used chants and sounding instruments to manipulate energy fields and bring about balance in the body. Pythagoras taught that sound was a creative force and that music held therapeutic benefits to the body. He claimed that he had learned this in the mystery schools of Egypt. If sound was held in high regard by the Egyptians it seems reasonable to assume that they would have incorporated this principle in their most impressive structure, the Great Pyramid.

Sound vibrations apparently were associated with creation, whether of the world or individual life patterns. "In the beginning was the Word." "Word" has been translated in various ways from "Logos," as law, archetypal patterns, etc. Philo wrote: "His image is the Word, a form more brilliant than fire. . . . The Logos is the vehicle by which God acts on the universe, and may be compared to the speech of man." The translations would seem to indicate the importance of vibration rather than the meaning of words.

A study of ancient cultures reveals that Chinese healers used "singing stones" in their rituals. These were thin, flat plates of jade which, when struck, gave off musical tones. They called the Great Tone of Nature, "Kung," which corresponds to our musical note of F. The Sufis consider "Hu" to be the creative sound. Tibetans consider the notes of A, F sharp, and G to be powerful sacred sounds. The sound of "AUM" is familiar to those persons acquainted with chants used in meditation. Our Christian

"Amen," was derived from the older "AUM," which represented all of the sounds that the human voice was capable of expressing and was, therefore, associated with the creative principle of the universe.

The ancient mystery schools associated rhythm with the body, melody with the emotions, and harmony lifted consciousness to spiritual awareness. It is interesting to note that persons hearing a sound or feeling a vibration while inside a pyramid have done so after directing their attention inward in efforts to elevate consciousness.

The woman, who many years ago introduced me (Schul) to metaphysical pursuits, has become the foremost exponent of the use of sound for therapeutic purposes. Laurel Elizabeth Keyes, a Denver author and lecturer, has developed a system of using the voices to bring balance to the body. Called "toning," she refers to it as the "lost word" once used by ancient healers.

While we were recently visiting her retreat in the Colorado mountains, she told us, "We create with words and with sound. Nearly all our actions and reactions result from words. It is generally accepted that we cannot think without words or symbols, and that our thinking is limited to them. Words are tools. It is important to have a good selection at our command. Beneath these words are the vibrations of the tone upon which they travel. Tone is the underlying force operating in our lives. To understand this, enhances our ability to create what we wish and to give form and substance to the ideas in our minds. Sound, I believe, is the meeting place of the abstract and the manifested idea."

The practice of toning began for Mrs. Keyes one day after a study group had left and she was standing alone in the room, enjoying the stillness that remains after such a meeting. "I noticed a sensation in my chest and throat, as though a force was rising, wanting to be released in sound. It was the feeling that might cause one to burst into song—for no known reason." (It is interesting to note that a number of persons have reported these same sensations while sitting in pyramids.)

"The feeling rose and subsided, but I was doing nothing to cause it," Mrs. Keyes continued. "It had a volition of its own and an apparent desire for expression. It was an odd experience to watch and feel, without making any effort to direct or control it. I found my lips parting, my mouth opening in an easy, relaxed manner. Unexpectedly, a sound bubbled up and a single syllable emerged: 'Ra.' I couldn't have been more astonished. I did not use Egyptian terms and we had not been discussing that culture in our study group. Why the sound took that form was as bewildering to me as if a foreign language might have sprung from my throat. I would liken it to a bird that had been caged all its life and suddenly found the cage door open.

"I did not take a deep breath, as a singer, but the note was sustained, as though supplied by a limitless source. And it went into heights I couldn't have reached normally since my voice is rather low.

"I decided I must have been in some phase of meditative state, so I taped the sound to evaluate it later in a more rational mood. When I listened to the recording the next day, I was amazed. It was not my voice. It belonged to my body, but I had never been able to use it in this manner before."

Mrs. Keyes, who has studied under a number of Eastern and Western teachers, found that toning burst through mental restrictions and released tensions. However, she soon discovered it provided more than that. Each time she toned, her body felt exhilarated; there was a feeling of wholeness and extreme well being.

Curious about the results, Mrs. Keyes turned to a friend with clairvoyant vision who had correctly diagnosed a number of ailments and asked her to watch the body-voice in expression. The woman saw the tone as a force with a swirling movement. It appeared to draw magnetic currents up from the earth through the feet and limbs, and rose in a spiral of light to the throat area.

"When I let the sound pass out, with no attempt to control it, it seemed to cleanse the entire body, releasing tensions in congested areas. Afterward, the body had a feeling of balance, like an engine that has been overhauled or a violin that has been tuned. The clairvoyant friend noticed that if, at first, I decided to direct the tone before it was free, the force collapsed back into the solar plexus area, where it tightened into feelings I might interpret as frustration, anxiety, and annoyance."

Following her newly discovered sound-idea through other cultures, Grecian, Egyptian, Persian, Indian, American Indian, and other primitive peoples, Mrs. Keyes found it was related to the oldest methods of healing, where two things prevailed in most ancient healing rituals: sound or chanting, and rhythmic body movements, either in dance or stomping.

Recent scientific theories developed along the lines of field theory have substantiated Mrs. Keyes's concept that every living thing has a field containing a pattern of perfection for manifestation. The pattern for a flower is in the seed, of the bird within the egg. Interference with the field will change the pattern, and illness or malformations will result.

She explains that as tone goes out, it collects substance from the world around it, forming a very tangible manifestation such as that seen by the cobweblike dust particles that collect in the pattern made by air currents from a furnace or window. When fine sand or sugar is sprinkled on a drumhead and put in contact with vibrations coming from a violin or piano, the granules take on various geometric patterns, evidence that sound can move matter and vibrations can cause changes in the molecular structure.

"Voice is vibrations," Mrs. Keyes stated. "It follows that the manner in which we use our voice is perhaps the most important factor in affecting the molecular structure of our body. Whining voices attract negative conditions. I found that people who speak in that manner are seldom free of problems. A person who has a hostile, condemning voice seems to attract violence, accidents, strokes, and heart attacks. By getting a person to change his tone of voice, he begins to change his life. I came to the conclusion that, if the willpower is controlled by the subconscious mind, the conscious use of the voice bypasses its hold and frees the will to be used however the mind directs."

By releasing tension and stimulating circulation and nerve energy in the body, Mrs. Keyes says she finds toning a natural way of healing. It releases a pattern of perfection within each person. These concepts parallel closely those proposed by Reich as regards orgone energy, ideas surrounding the multiwave oscillator, the Eeman screens, Edgar Cayce's wet-cell battery ideas, the theories of Dr. John Pierrakos, and reports of influence of pyramid power.

In order to better understand why thoughts and emotions affect the body, Mrs. Keyes refers to the colloidal structure (described in the chapter on healing). From atom, to molecule, to colloid, she points out that we are dealing with an energy form, easily influenced by vibration. She believes that toning, chanting, verbal prayer, electrotherapy, and the conscious use of the voice in calm and confidence give a needed positive charge to the miles of colloidal surface in the person.

One notable example of the effectiveness of toning deals with a woman who suffered from mononucleosis and had been sent home, in her own conviction, to die. "She was bedridden and so weak it was difficult for her to speak on the telephone," Mrs. Keyes said. She explained the toning idea to the woman and asked her to repeat simple sentences such as "I am going to get out of bed and do things I want to do," in a thrusting, positive way.

"Give it more thrust," Mrs. Keyes told her and finally, with some indignation, the woman responded, "I am thrusting my words out."

From that moment, Mrs. Keyes recalls, it seemed the force was reversed from negative to positive polarity. The next day, the woman was not only out of bed, but doing housework, and on the third day she drove to a nearby town to hear a lecture. There was no return of the illness. Apparently, changing her voice pattern began the change of her health.

But the problem may not always lie in the area of pain. One demonstration Mrs. Keyes remembers was a man who volunteered to have a headache relieved. "He had been suffering increasing and intensifying headaches," she recalls. "I started toning at his feet, and as the sound moved up, I traced it up to the inside of his leg, around the hip and to the back, up the back to his neck, and finally to his head. But I could not hold the sound in the head area because it couldn't get past a 'sticky' place in his foot.

"'I'm sorry,' I told him, 'but the trouble seems to be in your left foot.'

"'Nothing is wrong with my feet,' he insisted.

"'Would you please sit and press the inside of your foot arch. This is puzzling me very much.'

"He sat down. He was wearing flat, hard-soled sandals. He began probing the area of the arch and he let out a yell. 'Wow! That is sore.'

"He was a heavy man and wearing that type of sandal gave no support to his arch. Having found the source of the pain, we worked the sound all the way up, and he found the headache eased and, in a short time, was gone.

"When I demonstrate this technique," Mrs. Keyes added, "it is in no manner to imply I am a healer. It's only to convince people that sound they produce can have an effect upon their bodies."

One of Mrs. Keyes's first demonstrations was for a

young woman who stopped off in Denver feeling too ill to continue her flight to New York. According to Mrs. Keyes, she had the flu, a very stiff neck, and was very weak and unable to eat for several days. She also had a violent headache.

"Two of us toned for her for about fifteen minutes. I had been standing with my hands together, as in a prayer position, just under my chin. I felt a power build up in my hands as I toned, and I said to the woman, 'Ask what you will, but be sure you want it. I feel it will be released to you.'

"The woman didn't open her eyes. She mumbled 'I want to be free of this sickness and whatever caused it.' I opened my hands and held them, palms out toward her. She convulsed in the chair as though she had received an electric shock. She sat up and asked, 'What happened?'

"We could not answer. We stood with our mouths open, too surprised to speak. One thing that I had been taught was never to let fear in, no matter what you are doing. If we could have, we would have been frightened, but we just stood watching. The woman sat up straight, twisted her head from side to side freely, amazed. 'It's free; no pain. What has happened? I feel wonderful.' Then she stood up, walked about the room, and kept saying, 'I feel wonderful. I can't believe it! I don't believe in miracles. This can't have happened, but I feel wonderful, I never felt better. And I'm hungry.'

"The young woman said she felt as though she was walking on air. We drove her to the airport and, while we waited for her plane, she ordered a large lunch and ate it with relish. She told us later she retained that exalted feeling for the rest of the day and even into the next day, when, after working at her office, she felt normal again. All symptoms of the illness were gone."

It has been suggested by some that if one toned, resonating the sound in a particular part of the brain that controlled the afflicted area of the body, correction might be made through that means, a kind of sona-acupuncture of the brain.

When one has a pain in the body, Mrs. Keyes believes, one begins toning as low as the voice can reach, and slowly raises the pitch, as a siren sound rises.

"One will find there is a tone which resonates with pain and relieves tension," Mrs. Keyes stated. "This is all done with sensitivity to feeling. To get the idea, place your finger against your nose and hum, directing the sound to that spot. Notice the sensation. While this is not as definite in other parts of the body, it can be determined, and that is the tone that will relieve pain. Every pain has a companion tone and—by pulsating the tone softly for a time—the pain will be relieved or eliminated. It is an escape valve for the pain because it is breaking up the tension we label 'pain' and it brings new life energy to that place. It is an inner sonar message.

"Many times during public lectures I have asked someone in the audience who has a pain to come up and let this technique be demonstrated. As I stand facing the person, eyes closed and concentrating on the feeling of the sound, I start toning very low and slowly, letting the sound scan the body. When the sound returns to me from the afflicted area, I know it. It is an indescribable sensation—sticky and thick. There is no proper word for it, but it is noticeable. To help the person concentrate upon the exact area of distress, I ask him if the sound would seem more comfortable a little higher or lower. Then I pulsate the sound in a rhythmic manner until my body sighs. Then I reach a high note with the feeling of energizing the person's own source of energy and let the sound sweep down, flushing through the body perhaps two or three times."

To practice toning, Mrs. Keyes advices, stand erect, feet several inches apart. Stretch the arms high and let them drop back, shoulders swinging on the spine in perfect balance. The eyes must be closed. Then begin to look inward and feel. To counteract the usual tendency to cave in and bend forward, the torso must ride on the pelvic structure, with the hip bones protruding a little. Standing erect should cause no strain but give an easy, relaxed feeling.

"It is natural for the body to be held in a rigid position," Mrs. Keyes stated. "Let it sway slightly to get the feeling of life's pulsations within it."

"Feeling this magical process of aliveness within and around you, let your body speak," she states in her book on toning, *Toning—The Creative Power of the Voice,* published by DeVorss & Company. "Relax the jaws so the teeth are slightly parted. Let sound come up from it; not down upon it, but up, from your feet. Let the body groan. Encourage it to be vocal. Always start with low groans.

"Let the body groan as long as it likes. You may think you have nothing to groan about, but you'll be surprised. All the hurts you have received are buried in your subconscious, and groaning offers them release. Once the door is opened, repressed feelings begin to flow out. The groan may burst into protests, or the voice may soar off into birdlike singing or spontaneous outbursts of worship or prayer.

"Whatever happens, don't let the mind influence it," Mrs. Keyes cautions. "Make the sound obedient; be still. Watch, learn something of the host of this body in which you, as consciousness, are only a guest.

"The session may last only ten minutes but, when the body feels cleansed, a sigh will be released and you will know the body-voice is satisfied. The involuntary sigh is the signal. You feel good, as though something has been accomplished and you have brought yourself together into a harmonious whole.

"As soon as the sigh is released and cleansing for that time is complete, something must be offered to fill the emptied cup. If possible, sit down for a few moments and enjoy a book of inspiration. Whatever you do afterward, you will be aware that you have 'fastened the light' in yourself for the day."

Laurel Keyes's suggestion of swaying "to get the feeling of life's pulsations" may be a natural movement of various life forms responding to energy vibrations or to what some scientists have referred to as the "music of the hemispheres."

We experimented with the influence of musical tones on plants inside pyramids. Mrs. Keyes pointed out that sound can be either constructive or destructive. This concept would correspond to experiments with energy field intensities where—as described elsewhere in this book—forces can be beneficial or detrimental depending upon the intensity. This seemed to occur when we placed an oscillator inside a pyramid with the capacitor plate next to a plant. Producing 7,000 cycles per second, the plant next to the plate stopped the swaying movement. Another plant not in line with the capacitor plate but still inside the pyramid continued to gyrate but at a reduced rate. When the tone was reduced to 500 cycles per second, the plant next to the plate still remained motionless but the second plant started gyrating at twice the amplitude as before the sound was produced. The rate was then raised to 1,000 cycles per second and while the first plant still maintained suspended animation the second plant reached its optimum movement, according to our time-lapse films. Apparently, the 1,000 cycle rate was the "right" one for the second plant. However, rather than the musical tone being too intense for the motionless plant, as we first surmised, later experiments led us to believe that the inhibiting factors were the aluminum in the capacitor plate and, possibly, the permanent magnet in the speaker. For those interested in trying this experiment we would suggest that they place the speaker outside the pyramid but against the side in order to vibrate the pyramid without aluminum, magnets or electrical circuitry inside to inhibit or overload the energy field.

One of the more exciting experiments with the influence of sound on life forms was conducted by Mrs. Dorothy Retallack, a professional mezzo-soprano and the wife of a Denver physician. While completing some studies at Temple Buell College in Denver, Mrs. Retallack wanted to test her theory that music has an important influence on life forms. She chose plants as the medium for study and working with biology professor Francis F. Broman, Mrs. Retallack subjected a number of plants to rock music played by a local radio station and another group of experimental plants to classical music played by another station.

The plants leaned away from the rock music, some at 80-degree angles. Their root structures were shallow and also grew away from the music. The plant stems and leaves were small, fragile, and some died within a few days after the "treatment" started. Petunias refused to bloom. On the other hand, squash vines wrapped themselves around the radio playing harmonious classical and religious music. Six lovely blossoms appeared on the petunia plants. Roots of all plants were vigorous and the plants large and sturdy.

Excited about the results, Mrs. Retallack continued her experiments for another year. She enlarged the scope of her research, was careful to check all possible variables between experimental and control plants. The results were the same. Photographers from *Empire* magazine of the *Denver Post* photographed the growth of the plants and verified the findings.

We visited with Mrs. Retallack during a trip to Denver. "I just can't help but believe," she told us, "that my experiments have greater significance than just a study of plant growth. This is just another piece of evidence pointing to the interrelationships of all life forms. What is happening to plants cannot be isolated and this phenomena has application, I believe, to all life forms. I strongly feel that future investigations will reveal that some combination of harmonic sounds will improve human growth and heal illness. My research will find its place in the current investigations of energy fields. We have reason to believe the ancients possessed this knowledge; our task is to rediscover it."

Dr. Dale Kretchman, professor of horticulture at the Ohio Agriculture Experimental station, explains research such as that of Mrs. Retallack as indicative of high-frequency sounds altering the cells of growth regulators. Dr. George Milstein, retired dentist and lecturer on botanical subjects, tested Dr. Kretchman's theory under laboratory conditions and found that musically treated plants grow faster than control plants. Using his record album, "Music to Grow Plants By," released by Pickwick International, Dr. Milstein said that one plant bloomed in six months when it usually takes two years.

Indian literature abounds with references to plants responding to music and to test such legends Dr. T.C.N. Singh of Annamalai University in southern India initiated a series of experiments in the 1950s. He discovered that seeds germinated in one-third the normal time. In exploring means of increasing plant growth of seedlings, Dr. Singh found that overdoses of sound waves withered plants, but if a particular tune was played during a particular time each day, the plants responded with faster and healthier growth; also a high yield. Flutes or violins playing Indian classical music was the most effective, and it was also found that each plant had its own choice of tunes.

It was Dr. Singh's contention that music stimulates a higher production of oxygen, as much as 60 to 100 percent. As the plant's output of oxygen is directly proportional to the food manufactured by it, the stimulated plants are able to synthesize a larger amount of nourishment than the control plants. After many years of experimentation, Dr. Singh concluded that repeated musical stimulation brings about positive changes in the chromosome arrangement of certain plant cells.

Brett L. Bolton quotes Dr. Singh in *The Secret Power of Plants* as saying, "After all, sound is not a myth; it is a definite, measurable, physical phenomena charged with energy, like the light and heat that so abundantly affect plant metabolism and growth."

The Department of Agriculture of the Indian state of Pondicherry started experimenting with Dr. Singh's concepts in 1958 in efforts to improve crops. Tests of rice, sugar, and tapioca revealed an astonishing increase of between 28 and 61 percent of the experimental crops over the control ones. The yield of straw was increased as much as 75 percent.

Hearing of Dr. Singh's work, George E. Smith, a research scientist with the Mangelsdorf Seed Company of St. Louis, decided to test the Indian's theories in his company's greenhouses. He planted several flats of corn and soybeans. The control plants were placed in a greenhouse without the benefit of music and the experimental plants were placed in a separate greenhouse in which a phonograph played Gershwin's "Rhapsody in Blue" 24 hours a day for 20 days. The Gershwin plants sprouted earlier and grew larger than the control plants. The next experiment Smith performed in the fields. "Rhapsody in Blue," along with several other songs were played to the experimental plants via a loudspeaker on top of a tall pole. Once again, germination occurred earlier, plant growth was larger and the treated corn outyielded the control corn by 20 bushels to the acre. Subsequent experiments have confirmed the results.

"Experiments have shown that a short burst of light energy can 'wake up' a plant and make it grow even in darkness," Bolton quoted Smith as saying. He added, "This, of course, has no bearing on my experiments, but it does indicate that bursts of energy in various forms may touch off unique effects of which we aren't aware."

Sound, of course, is one division or portion of a known spectrum of energy among which there may well be a vast range of spectrums yet undiscovered. While the Bible and other ancient literature refers to the use of sound, and the ancient Greeks felt it was necessary to make music in their gymnasiums to balance and temper the mind and soul, centuries have slipped by without sound being taken seriously except by way of pleasure and verbal communication. But Indian fakirs still play tunes to control their captured cobras, weightlifters still grunt before they lift, a practitioner of mantram yoga continues to repeat his chant over and over again, and a karate expert still gives a sharp cry before he strikes, all releasing and giving direction to an energy force. Likely they use sound not because they have a theory but because they have discovered it works for them. Maybe the rest of us, demonstrating that sound works with our plants and pyramids, will continue to ask why long enough that someday we will understand the reason the Egyptian-trained Pythagoras insisted that in his schools various kinds of music were to be used for various activities. More pieces of the puzzle are being collected every day.

10. THE PYRAMID & ALTERED STATES OF CONSCIOUSNESS

Stillness built ominous walls around me; I (Schul) was cut off, separated from my reality checks, and I touched my face, my legs, the floor on which I sat, to orient myself in space. It retreated and came back to press upon me. The stillness grew, became heavier, and finally shouted at me from its anti-sound existence. I listened. My whole being became the verb *listen*. And then I wasn't.

How long I sat there, curled yoga style, in the darkness I do not know. All was suspended, but from somewhere there slipped in a fragment of time and some small rent in space and I was again. It was me, I knew that, remembered that, and I constructed me again . . . me on a concrete floor, inside a plastic pyramid, inside a wooden building, inside a garden, inside a universe. A car passed in the street outside and not too distant two dogs informed one another of certain territorial rights. I collected reality items from outside, the car and then another, the dogs, gusts of wind breathing heavily through the leaves of the elms.

Once collected, I found I could release the items and settle within myself again. The stillness came back but this time to share rather than demand and a great, permeating sense of contentment seemed to envelope me. I was and would remain; no other source for the peacefulness than this.

After a while I became aware that I had moved. I was standing and directly in front of me, my feet touching the base, was the Great Pyramid of Gizeh. This realization did not seem strange to me but I was nearly overcome, however, by the immensity of the mountain. I stood in awe for some time, looking up at its apex. Quite suddenly, I was inside the pyramid. It was not a room or passageway in which I found myself and yet I did not seem encased in stone and while definitely within the structure I could still look up and see the apex. Just as quickly, that scene changed and I was inside the King's Chamber. I went forward to the stone sarcophagus and lay down within it, seemingly as a matter of course, closed my eyes, breathed deeply, and waited. Without opening my eyes, I became aware that there were several entities in attendance. They were sending silent messages to me. I lifted out of my body and hovered about the chamber and saw my body in the coffer but was disinterested in it. I seemed to be moving out of the chamber and toward another section of the pyramid, but just as suddenly as before the scene changed. It was no longer the Great Pyramid; it was a nine-foot plastic model. This metamorphosis startled me; the other had seemed so real.

I struggled for several minutes with my disappointment. As I was planning on spending the night inside the pyramid, I lay down on the cot. Yet I could not sleep as I tried to understand what had happened to me. Clearly, I had not been asleep and dreaming, for the physical signs of entering and coming out of sleep were not present. I was equally sure it had not been a matter of fantasizing, for I had not gone through the usual mental constructs. I had been meditating at the time and the most plausible explanation seemed to be an experience of mental projection. If it was an out-of-the-body experience, it was as real on one level as an actual physical experience.

Paul Brunton's account of his night alone in the Great Pyramid kept coming back to me. In the early 1930s writer-philosopher Dr. Paul Brunton was granted the highly unprecedented privilege of spending the night inside the Pyramid. He tells of the experience in *A Search in Secret Egypt*. As far as is known no one had stayed overnight in the Pyramid for a hundred years, nor has anyone since Brunton. He was told that it was not allowed and only gained permission after great persistence. It is a commonly held belief of the natives of the area, as well as many others, that the Pyramid is haunted. Strange tales have been told through the ages of beings within who come alive at night and stalk the passageways. Those daring to stay after sunset invite the curse of the pharoahs and if they should by chance live through the ordeal they would be hopelessly insane.

It is the custom to lock the iron gate of the entrance at sundown and Brunton was told that no exception could be made. Once inside, he was virtually a prisoner during the hours of darkness. He moved through the narrow passageways, confronted by large bats and looming unexpected shadows of himself cast by his flashlight beam. He arrived in the King's Chamber, sat down beside the coffinlike sarcophagus, turned off the light, and waited.

He achieved a passive, receptive state of mind and determined to hold the contemplative state throughout the long night.

The atmosphere of the room became very real to him, and the feeling grew that he was not alone, "that something animate and living was throbbing into existence. . . . Quickly I found that the sensing of invisible life around me rapidly rose into complete certainty.". .

Brunton struggled with his feelings of fear and the "nameless dread" that flickered into his heart, and tried to maintain his meditative position on the floor. "Shadows began to flit to and fro in the shadowless room; gradually these took more definite shape, and malevolent countenances appeared suddenly quite close to my own face. Sinister images rose plainly before my mind's eye. Then a dark apparition advanced, looked at me with fixed sinister regard and raised its hands in a gesture of menace, as though seeking to inspire me with awe. . . ."

Every effort seemed to be made to drive him from his vigil. "At last the climax came. Monstrous elemental creations, evil horrors of the underworld, forms of grotesque, insane, uncouth and fiendish aspect gathered around me and afflicted me with unimaginable repulsion. In a few minutes I lived through something which will leave a remembered record behind for all time. That incredible scene remains vividly photographed upon my memory. . . ."

But the end came with "startling suddenness." All became quiet within the stone vault. Then a new presence made itself known. The atmosphere changed from one of foreboding and evil to one of pureness and sanity. Brunton experienced the entrance of a friendly and benevolent being and then another. They approached him and were seen as tall, white-robed figures. "Indeed, they looked more than men, bearing the bright mien of demi-gods; for their faces were set in unique cloistral calm."

After he was observed for some time, Brunton was told that he should not have come, that he should "follow the path appointed for mortal feet." When he stated that he had to follow the path he had chosen and could not be persuaded to leave, the being whom he likened to an Egyptian high priest spoke to him. "So be it. Thou hast chosen. Abide by thy choice for there is now no recall. Farewell."

When the first figure was gone, the second figure moved closer. "My son," he said, "the mighty lords of the secret powers have taken thee into their hands. Thou art to be led into the Hall of Learning tonight." He was told to stretch out upon the stone sarcophagus; his body became numb as an iciness passed from his feet throughout his body. When all awareness seemed to rest in the head, he seemed to be caught up in a whirlwind, and passing upward through a narrow hole, "I lept into the unknown—I was Free!"

Out of his body, a "phantom . . . showing up the wallstones in a soft moonbeamlike light," Brunton was then allegedly taken to other parts of the Pyramid where he was instructed by his host. While fragments of the teachings were offered the reader, one has the distinct impression that there were many secret insights that Brunton either chose not to divulge or was so instructed. Reading Brunton's later books, particularly *The Wisdom of the Overself,* one cannot help but be stirred by the profundity of his message. One wonders, then, if the messages of this strange night are being offered. Brunton never says. Yet, one of the instructions given him, which he does share, may in a very real way sum up all instructions: ". . . The mystery of the Great Pyramid is the mystery of thine own self. The secret chambers and ancient records are all contained in thine own nature. . . ."

Sitting there in my own small darkness, the setting much less romantic than Brunton's, I kept telling myself that I was harboring some grandiose hallucination, that it was dramatic of me to compare in any manner my experience with his. But there it was. I could not erase the vividness of what to me had seemed utterly real at the time it was being experienced. I, too, had gone within myself and where, I asked, does any experience occur but within oneself? Brunton's experience did not occur to the stone, but within himself; could mine be denied because it happened at another place on earth and within a structure of different materials?

In the gloomy vault directly above the King's Chamber in the Great Pyramid one man in recent history actually lived. Captain G. B. Caviglia was a man of mystery. In the 1830s Caviglia saw the pyramids on the Gizeh plain and became enamoured of their mystique. Master of a Maltese merchant vessel, he gave up the sea and the Great Pyramid became his new mistress. He cleaned out the bat excrement from Davison's Chamber (named after Nathaniel Davison who discovered the room around 1765) and set up housekeeping in the three-foot high room.

Alexander William Crawford (Lord Lindsay), who knew Caviglia in Cairo, described the Italian as deeply religious but a very strange man. Crawford wrote: "Caviglia told me that he had pushed his studies in magic, animal magnetism, etc., to an extent which nearly killed him . . . to the very verge, he said of what is forbidden man to know, and it was only the purity of his intentions which saved him." Crawford offers us no further elaboration on this, and Caviglia, who died years later in Paris, left no written record of his experiences.

One other encounter with the mind-altering properties of the King's Chamber should be mentioned. It was brief, but it may have altered history; so great was its impact on the mind of a man who held for a time control of several nations. In 1798 Napoleon Bonaparte conquered Egypt. He visited the Great Pyramid, and upon entering the King's Chamber asked to be left alone for a time.

Peter Tompkins tells of the incident in *Secrets of the Great Pyramid*. "Coming out, the general is said to have been very pale and impressed. When an aide asked him in a jocular tone if he had witnessed anything mysterious, Bonaparte replied abruptly that he had no comment, adding in a gentler voice that he never wanted the incident mentioned again.

"Many years later, when he was emperor, Napoleon continued to refuse to speak of this strange occurrence in the Pyramid, merely hinting that he had received some presage of his destiny. At St. Helena, just before the end, he seems to have been on the point of confiding to Las Cases, but instead shook his head, saying, 'No. What's the use. You'd never believe me.'"

There are other strange tales to be told of experiences within the Great Pyramid. But of greater significance to most of us are the personal accounts of those who have experienced something different or unusual within the space of pyramid replicas. These experiences are to be easily obtained by anyone willing to build or borrow a large enough pyramid to sit, stand, or lie down in. These experiences, of course, will be of a subjective nature. Endeavoring to unravel their source, it can be said that the observer is imagining, fantasizing, hallucinating, fabricating the experience. True, and the same can be said for Brunton's experience, or for that matter, any personal experience. We can become deeply involved in philosophical discourses on the nature of reality and nonordinary realities. But, in the final analysis, those experiences to which we give the greatest credence are those that we share in some fashion with others.

We are not devoid of these commonly shared experiences when we turn to the reports of those who have spent brief and extended periods within pyramid models. We have visited with a number of these individuals and discovered that their experiences were related, without their having any previous knowledge of the experiences of others. A number of persons, who had no acquaintance with pyramids, were asked to meditate or just to sit for a time inside a pyramid and to tell us what they felt or thought afterward.

The common denominators were feelings of solitude, peace, and greater detachment from the world and less concern over physical matters. Because of these feelings, those familiar with meditation stated they felt less distracted, more removed, and could more easily center within themselves. While there were those who said they felt no difference inside than outside the pyramid, they were the exceptions. Most experienced something if it was nothing more than a sense of calmness or mild euphoria. Relaxation was a commonly reported phenomena, as were feelings of renewed energy or "being charged."

"When I meditated inside the pyramid, I felt a weight or force being moved through my body, starting at the top of the head and moving down through the shoulders, the body, and into the legs," Carl Waldon told us. "The next day there was a particular clearness of thought, much more energy, and an ability to know and understand."

"There was a keen awareness of a strong heart beat and seemingly a movement inside. My head seemed to be pulled toward the apex and there was a desire to place my hands together in a prayer poise," Lora Lee Camp stated.

Anna Maye Ingram, unaware of Camp's reaction, told us, "The first impression was peaceful silence. After some minutes there seemed to be a heavy pressure around me, holding or pushing me deep into the chair. There seemed to be an enlargement of the heart and I was very aware of my heart. There was a power of some kind going to the heart, or coming from the heart. The entire body seemed to take on a vibration—a tingle—as if one had been holding onto a machine that was vibrating very fast."

Movie actress Gloria Swanson has stated that she feels a "tingling" when she sleeps with a small pyramid beneath her bed. In *Pyramid Power* Max Toth and Greg Nielsen state: "Another interesting observation made by many of the participants in these experiments was when they raised their hands into the apex, they experienced a prickling sensation, as if tiny needles were being stuck into the extremity."

The "tingling" sensations are reminiscent of statements made by persons subjected to the energy force of the multiwave oscillator or the Reich orgone accumulator. Occasionally one hears of someone making a similar comment about acupuncture.

Regarding reports of unusual sensations in the heart, Toth and Nielson comment: "Allegedly, the most benefi- cient energies inside the pyramid are focused within the so-called heart center. This is the spot which is probably the 'safest' for the incubation of thought-forms. However, it has been suggested that different thought-forms might best be incubated at different spots in order for the person inside the pyramid to receive the energy most advanta- geous in fulfilling the specific thought-form."

Persons using pyramid structures in which to meditate on a regular basis have claimed they experience serenity and an integration with cosmic forces. Several have re- ported that they receive spiritual impressions while inside the pyramid and upon leaving psychic perceptions seem to flood their consciousness.

Tenny Hale, an Oregon psychic-sensitive, claims that during heightened awareness, brought on by a seven-day fast and intense meditation, she was instructed to use a pyramid for achieving beneficial altered states of con- sciousness and to improve her already existing powers of extrasensory perception. Upon leaving her pyramid fol- lowing meditation exercises, she claims that psychic im- pressions fill her mind. On one occasion she went to her typewriter and typed 100 different prophecies. According to newspaper and magazine reports, Mrs. Hale has been accurate on a number of psychic revelations.

Two psychic researchers lived for a time in a large wooden pyramid in Florida. Rev. Ron Oesterbro and Mrs. Rose Stephens subsisted mainly on fruit juices and spent a great deal of time in meditation. After a month the couple reported receiving messages on physical cures, the origin and purpose of man, and information of a prophetic nature.

For the past year I (Pettit) have slept two nights a week in one of our pyramids. I sincerely believe that this experience has contributed to my good health and an increase in energy. I look forward to sleeping in the pyramid because of the serenity and peaceful solitude I have found there. It is very difficult to maintain a state of tension while inside the pyramid, and this feeling of greater ease has been increasingly extended throughout the day.

Dreaming, of course, is one state of awareness, and I have noticed that in recent months my dreams have become clearer and more vivid. A number have taken on qualities of reality of the normal waking state. Recently a dream in which a small baby was laughing seemed to unfold a panorama of man's evolution. The laughing infant appeared to be a graphic way of illustrating the nature of man's sojourn on this planet; the baby was quite an old soul but had appeared once again in the form of a child.

On another occasion, while lying on the cot in the pyramid, in the twilight zone between sleep and wakefulness, I saw a wide, white ribbon of road lined with stately trees winding through lush farmland. I seemed to be driving some sort of blue and white vehicle. It pulled into what I knew to be the sanitation department's garbage and refuse area, but it was beautifully landscaped, approximately one-half mile wide and one mile long.

In front of me were eight gleaming pyramids, each painted a different color of distinct pastel. I seemed to know that the pyramids were around 250 feet tall and with bases 375-foot square.

Narrower roads branched off the main road and served as access routes to the pyramids. Each of the roads were of colored concrete matching the hue of the pyramid to which they led. The pyramid in use at this time was number three, counting from the east. I turned onto the salmon-colored road and drove toward the pyramid of that color. I could smell the delightful scent of growing plants and flowers lining the road, but there was no unpleasant odor of garbage.

I backed the vehicle to the base of the pyramid and dumped my load onto an extended conveyor belt, which carried the refuse into the pyramid. Refuse was piled in a 160-foot square within the pyramid and would remain there for seven weeks to be dehydrated and cleaned of harmful bacteria. It would then be carried by an underground conveyor-belt system to nearby plants for final processing where various materials would be separated, some for building uses, some for use in road construction, and the organic matter for fertilizer.

The vision was very real to me, and I can still see it in some detail.

My experience of vivid visual imagery apparently is not uncommon to those who have spent any time at all inside pyramids. They have reported increased memory recall and, allegedly, views of past incarnations.

Inez Pettit has spent considerable time inside a pyramid, relaxing on a chaise lounge for one to two hours at a time. There she seems to pass into a half-sleep state, still conscious of the world about her while the subjective world within takes on its own reality.

On one of these occasions she found herself floating above a large city. It was beautifully planned, she said, and it seemed to glow in a rainbow light. On each of the four sides of the city were huge pyramids of polished stone. The cap-stones of the pyramids appeared to be of crystal from which came a soft but brilliant glow. She said she knew the pyramids served to produce the energy power for the city.

The people of the city wore long robes of caftan type;

the men in solids and stripes and the women in flowered robes. They appeared quite tall, from 10 to 15 feet. All seemed particularly alive, cheerful, laughing.

"I could see no ground-level vehicles. Instead there were wide moving walks crisscrossing throughout the city," Inez said. "The walks were green in color and soft to the feet like grass. They moved slowly so that the people could enjoy the scenery, and there were quite a large number of gardens about the size of city blocks. The moving walks had stone benches at intervals.

"I could hear the conversations, which was typical of most groups today, talk of children, homes, different interests and pursuits. I heard one woman remark to another that this was her birthday and she was not too happy at being middle-aged at 492 years. The other woman remarked, 'Just wait until you reach 900 or so and then you can start feeling old.'

"The houses were all the same size, looking like square cubicles built of some kind of translucent material. There were buildings other than houses, none of them very tall, not more than three or four stories. I went into one of the houses. All I saw was one huge room with stone upholstered couches and benches. One wall of the room was definitely an entertainment and communications center. When they wanted to see what we call movies, they would somehow cause the whole wall to go opaque and the entertainment would start, or if they wanted to communicate with someone, the person would appear on the wall and talk with them. I really don't know how they accomplished these things. I didn't see any buttons or knobs to push or turn. Perhaps they just mentally willed these activities into existence.

"It kept worrying me that no one seemed to be working. Some of the buildings must have been hobby centers for arts and crafts. Another thing, I saw no washers or dryers or any type of washroom; no kitchens, baths, or tables and chairs, or anything like that. I saw no one eat-ing anything. They were all perfectly clean and their clothing was immaculate. There were all sorts of questions in my mind to which there seemed no answers.

"There was a form of vehicle traffic for the city, all of it in the air, tear-shaped translucent ships that darted about over the city with incredible speed. When they landed they came straight down and sat on the roofs. The ships seemed to have no visible means of locomotion and made no sound. It seemed that when they were in the city, they automatically received energy from the pyramids. However, there were times when they needed to replenish the power. This was when they wanted to travel to another city or out into space. Then the ships would hover above one of the pyramids at the apex for a relatively short period of time to acquire the extra power for their journey. The time of recharging depended on the distance they were to travel.

"After seeing several of the ships leaving the pyramid power-zones and dart out into space, I slowly came out of my half-sleep. The vision was particularly clear and I feel certain that I will remember it for a long time. But though I have returned to the pyramid many times since, and have had other interesting experiences, I have never returned to the rainbow city."

As regards dreams, it is interesting to note that Mark Lehner, in an article, "Egypt—Reflections on a Tour," written for a recent issue of the *A.R.E. Journal*, tells of visiting with a very old Arab guide who told him that he had gone many times to a hole in the head of the Sphinx to dream. When Lehner asked him what he dreamed about, the guide replied, "I dream about the old people."

"The old people?" Lehner asked. "What do you see them doing?"

"Running about, working, building," and he imitated persons working with hammer and chisel. "The Sphinx is the best place for dreams."

People have reported that a daily dose of pyramid

power improves concentration. It apparently worked in one case at least. A college student of our acquaintance was having difficulty concentrating on his studies. We made a pyramid for his bedroom large enough for him to sit in. He started meditating in it each evening and told us that his grades had vastly improved. The student, Dave Wilcox, stated that he had found new security and confidence in himself. "There is great harmony inside the pyramid," he said. "I feel a oneness and closeness with the source. My yoga teacher has tried meditating in the pyramid and gets high in a very short time."

The *National Enquirer,* January 13, 1974, quoted Hollywood star James Coburn: "I firmly believe in pyramid power. I crawl inside my pyramid tent, sit in a yoga position, and does it work! It gives off a definite feeling and sensation. It creates an atmosphere . . . that makes it easier to meditate. It closes out all interference. I meditate in there every day, between fifteen minutes to an hour."

Pyramid hats worn to obtain altered states of consciousness have been suggested by Karel Drbal. Drbal was the Czechoslovakian radio engineer who launched the new pyramidia when his research with pyramid models was discussed in the Schroeder and Ostrander bestseller, *Psychic Discoveries Behind the Iron Curtain.*

Drbal wondered why the hats of sorcerers and witches were cone-shaped, and he tried a few experiments with pyramid-shaped hats. Several of his subjects reported feeling an influx of spiraling energy coming down from the top of the hat. "Apparently," Drbal was quoted as saying, "the pyramid acts like a kind of cosmic antenna tuning into sources of energy of vaster intensity and then focusing it into its center."

Toth and Nielsen suggest that the ancient Egyptian priests may have worn their pyramid-shaped hats when worshipping their sun god, Ra, because the hats may have focused electromagnetic energy from the sun or from some higher metaphysical plane. Such a possibility is also suggested by J. Furlong in *Rivers of Life*.

Perhaps the old practice of putting a dunce hat on a student who wasn't shaping up too well wasn't so much a matter of holding him out to ridicule as it was to send him some mental energy. We might hypothesize that the practice was viewed as a means of helping the child to get back into focus, re-centered, to concentrate, re-aligned with the source.

Jane Roberts, author of the *Seth* series, doesn't use a dunce hat of physical materials, but she writes that under certain conditions, "I got the feeling that a cone came down just over my head. I didn't think that an actual physical cone was there, but the idea of shape was definite. The wide end was about the size of my head, with the narrow part on top like a pyramid."

The E.S.P. Laboratory, Los Angeles, has been conducting experiments with the pyramid shape being used as an incubator for thought-forms. It is hypothesized that the pyramid form serves as a geometric amplifier which strengthens the request or desire of the individual making the thought-form.

According to the laboratory's director, Al Manning, a small pyramid is used along with triangular pieces of paper. The paper sheets are of four colors: yellow for intuition; orange for mental clarity; blue for healing; and green for love. The experimenter chooses one of the colors, appropriate for his designs, and writes on the triangular sheet a specific request or goal.

The paper is then held between the hands while a chant —one's own or one given by the organization—is repeated twice. The apex is then folded down to the base and the bottom folded over to make a triangle. The hands are then held above the triangle and the chant repeated again. This last step should be done with the paper lying on the base of the pyramid. The pyramid is then placed back on its base—always aligned on the north-south axis—and the incubation period has begun. Manning suggests that it takes between three and nine days for the thought-form to complete its "gestation period." During this period of time, the process is strengthened by chanting and holding the thought-form mentally. One should focus on the thought-form through the north side of the pyramid once a day, Manning states.

The experimenter removes the pyramid from its base and takes out the triangular sheet of paper when he feels that the incubation period has been completed. The paper is unfolded; a lower corner of the paper is grasped and the triangle is set on fire. The completely devoured ashes are placed in a fireproof receptacle kept at hand during the proceedings.

It is believed that the procedure of burning the paper is for the purpose of releasing the thought-form in order that it may accomplish its mission. Once the thought-form is liberated, the experimenter awaits the results believing that the fire has released a fully charged thought-form that will become manifest.

The exercise sounds magical and bizarre, but members of the organization throughout the world claim that their requests have been fulfilled.

The E.S.P. Laboratory has constructed several large pyramids to research the effects of pyramid energy on energy centers in the human body. They draw parallels between the locations of energy centers in the pyramid structure and those in the body. Their research would indicate that the energy in the higher parts of the pyramid is of a higher frequency, whereas the lower regions produce a warm and somewhat soothing feeling.

These experimenters have reported that there are some spots within the pyramids that are not beneficial, that sitting or lying at particular spots may cause headaches. Apparently, such experiences have been recorded by persons unaware of the reactions of other experimenters.

Talk of good spots and bad spots reminds one of Carlos Castaneda's counsel by Don Juan. He is told that there are places of personal power, an individual's own special piece of earth where he can be strong and immune. Then, there are other spots that can destroy.

Animals seem to be aware of these special places. They search until they find them and return again and again. Regardless of how much one tries, for example, to make a dog comfortable, if the place is not right, he will not rest there. He will drag the bedding, or whatever, to a different spot.

Our experiments with plants would seem to indicate that all locations within the pyramid are not equal. And we have found that subjects asked to relax or meditate within a pyramid will usually shift around somewhat until they feel comfortable. It would seem that the atmosphere or field within the pyramid is more intense than on the outside. When the "spot" is right, it is more pleasurable, calming, and enhancing than one might experience otherwise, but when it is wrong, it is really wrong.

We have been told that there are special energy vortices on earth, that these were known and used by the ancients. Some were healing places, some holy places. One wonders, then, if a device or structure so designed as to gather or amplify these special energy fields wouldn't create a miniature universe within themselves? If so, perhaps the pyramids are offering us more answers than we have thus far suspected.

11. ESOTERIC GEOMETRY & ENERGY GRIDS

The science and philosophy of the ancient world was based on numbers and geometry, and it is difficult to believe that the greatest monument of the ages, whose design is of all the most carefully executed and most geometrically conceived, wouldn't illustrate the highest knowledge of its age.

It is exciting to speculate that the Great Pyramid was constructed as a highly sophisticated scientific instrument, an exact scale model of the world, by an Egyptian culture —or possibly pre-Egyptian—far more advanced than has generally been believed. This theory demonstrates that the Pyramid incorporated the basic formula of the universe and was designed to help man orient himself in the cosmos and to apply definitive measurements to time and space.

Dr. Livio C. Stecchini, a specialist in the history of measurement and quantitative science and presently serving as professor of ancient history at William Patterson

College in New Jersey, has been able to demonstrate that at least as early as 2800 B.C. the Egyptians could measure latitude and longitude quite accurately, an ability not duplicated in our era until the eighteenth century. These ancient scientists knew the circumference of the earth precisely and the length of their own country to the cubit, along with the geographical coordinates of all the major points in their realm from the Mediterranean to the equator. In order to accomplish this, according to Stecchini, the Egyptians were able to make astronomical observations with the kind of exactness provided by the modern telescope and chronometer.

Stecchini, who wrote an extensive and informative appendix entitled "Notes on the Relation of Ancient Measures to the Great Pyramid," for Tompkins's book, *Secrets of the Great Pyramid,* did a twenty-year study of the mathematical and astronomical data contained in the cuneiform tablets of the ancient Sumerians and Babylonians. As a result of his studies of the stepped ziggurats of the Middle East and the pyramids, he was able to show that these structures incorporated the basic techniques for mapping the structure and design of the heavens and for mapping the terrestial hemisphere. The structures also reveal a high level of mathematics, capable of resolving problems of trigonometry, according to Stecchini.

The apex of the Great Pyramid corresponds to the pole, and the perimeter to the equator, with both in exact scale. It is apparent that each side of the Pyramid was designed to correspond to one curved quarter of the northern hemisphere, or a spherical quadrant of 90 degrees.

In order to project a spherical quadrant onto a flat triangle correctly, the arc of the quadrant must be the same length as the base of the triangle, and both must have the same height. This happens to be the case, Tompkins explains, only with a cross section or meridian bisection of the Great Pyramid. Its slope angle gives the Pi relation between height and base. When viewed from the side, the Pyramid's projection is such that the laws of perspection reduce the actual area of a face to the correct size for the projection. This is the Pyramid's cross section. What one actually sees is the correct triangle.

The Greek historian Merodotus was told by the Egyptian priests that the Pyramid was planned in such a way that the area of each of its faces was equal to the square of its height. It is now evident that this was the key to the Pyramid's geometrical and mathematical secret. This information reveals that the Pyramid was designed to incorporate not only the Pi proportion but the constant proportion known during the Rennaissance as the Golden Section, or Phi, or 1.618.

Phi is an unending ratio. This mystical formula is as old as history and is a fascinating system of numers. It is a summation series and has been called the Fibonaci series. Succeeding terms beginning with one are obtained by adding together the two preceding terms, as follows: 1, 2, 3, 5, 8, 13, 21, 34, 55, 89, 144, 233, and so on. Phi, or 1.618, is obtained by dividing any one term of the summation series by its predecessor. The terms move closer to Phi when the numbers are larger. Thus three divided by two is 1.5; thirteen divided by eight is 1.625; 233 divided by 144 is 1.6180555.

Phi has also been called the Sacred Cut because it is the exact ratio in which a line AC can be divided by B in such a way that AC/AB equals 1.618 and is the same as AB/BC equals 1.618. This ratio was used by Renaissance artists as it was considered the most aesthetic proportion. It is said that these proportions occur throughout nature. The body of man is said to be divided by this ratio, and the sacred five-pointed star's diagonals divide each other by this same ratio. The Great Pyramid, using the Golden Section, becomes an effective system for translating spherical areas into flat areas.

The Egyptians used a measuring unit known as a cubit.

Evidently the Egyptian cubit was formulated by taking one-thousandth of the distance the earth travels at the equator in one second. The designers of the Great Pyramid made the base length the distance the earth travels in one-half a second. The cubit was equal to one-thousandth of a second of time, and the foot was equal to one-thousandth of a second of arc.

It now seems evident that the ancient scientists computed the polar circumference of the earth by using the sun and the shadows cast by obelisks. In order to determine the circumference of the earth at the equator, the builders observed the passage of stars across fixed points of the obelisks. To figure the polar circumference all they needed do was measure the distance between two obelisks several miles apart and the difference in the shadows cast by the obelisks.

There was no need to measure vast distances. The fraction of arc separating any two meridian obelisks, hence the difference in latitude, could be determined by the comparison of the obelisk's shadow to its height when measured at the moment of the solstice or equinox.

In order to determine the circumference of the earth at the equator, Tompkins explains that an observer at the base of an obelisk at the thirtieth parallel could signal the appearance of a zenith star on the eastern horizon to another observer at a measured distance away where the tip of the obelisk would be on the horizon. Determining the interval of time between the appearance of the star to the two observers, and knowing that the earth rotates through 1,296,000 seconds of arc in 86,400 seconds (24 hours) of time, the equatorial circumference of the earth could be computed.

The evidence that the Great Pyramid was constructed in such a manner to imply squaring the circle and cubing the sphere would seem to indicate that the builders were saying that the static geometry of angles could be shifted to the dynamic geometry of curves. The Pyramid can be seen as a cone and the cube can be seen as a sphere. According to Henry Monteith, who contributed an essay, "Geometry of the Great Pyramid," to *Pyramid Power,* the cone is a perfect representation of the dynamic concentration of energy. This would seem to imply that the shape of the cone is connected with creation in some manner.

In the chapter describing our experiments with plants inside pyramids, mention is made of testing the growth of seedlings inside several different goemetrical structures. We found that plants grow faster inside cone-shaped containers than inside pyramids. Plants also grew faster at the apex of the pyramid than at the level of the King's Chamber, which is one-third the distance from the base to the apex.

Newton explained that for every action there is an equal and opposite reaction. As it is assumed that the universe must always be in perfect balance, it can also be assumed that there must be a reaction or counterpart to all perceived forces and bodies. In the above mentioned paper, Monteith points out that in physics it is understood that if there is a positive charge located at some distance above ground, one can determine the field between the charge and ground by assuming there is another charge, which is negative, located at equal distance below ground. In other words, according to Monteith, when a positive charge is present, a negative charge is also implicitly present, although it is not physically present. He speculates that there is implicitly present one or more anti-pyramids to the Great Pyramid.

It should be remembered that the Great Pyramid is not symmetrical. The sides do not form equilateral triangles. Further, the sides of the stone structure are slightly indented. This has been noted by William Flinders Petric in his measurements, even though the indention is not visible to the human eye. This was confirmed by an aerial photograph taken by British Brigadia P.R.C. Groves.

The slight hollowing of the sides is significant inasmuch as it accounts for what appeared to be small errors by the Egyptians in mathematical and geometrical determinations. However, of perhaps greater importance, the indentions may have been required in order for the Great Pyramid to serve as an energy field resonator or generator. Our experiments with pyramid models, including ones with mirrored sides, indicate that if the sides are slightly indented to throw an entering energy field off the straight line upon striking the opposite side and, thus, was reflected, the lines of force tend to be directed toward the center of the pyramid. The behavior of visible light rays were used as a model in our experiments.

The nonsymmetrical design of the Pyramid would seem to imply two directions of thought projection, one toward the apex, which Monteith views as representing material creation, and the other toward the base and destruction. The anti-construction pyramid is an inverted pyramid located above the apex of the physical pyramid and brings about creation. The anti-destruction pyramid is base-to-base with its physical pyramid and is located below the ground. It effects expansion and death of that which has been created. Construction and destruction interact cyclically with each other, according to Monteith.

It is believed that one of the primary purposes of asymmetry in nature is to establish the necessary conditions to initiate motion. In a paper entitled "Possibility of Experimental Study of the Properties of Time," Nikolai Kozyrev proposes that time has the ability to decrease the entropy of a system, although the change usually goes unnoticed. However, in the Great Pyramid the action of time has been amplified as a result of its shape, and this allows it to preserve organic matter. "Time-flow and Bioplasma are just different terms used to describe the same mysterious force which is responsible for the creation and maintenance of all material systems," Kozyrev states. He adds, "Bioplasma has the ability to increase the energy of a system but is unable to affect the momentum of a system."

It is believed that bioplasma may have properties which are opposite those of nuclear energy. Dr. Wilhelm Reich experimented with this concept and refers to it as "The Oranur Experiment" in his book, *Cosmic Superimposition*. He discovered that bioplasma responded violently with radioactive materials and produced a by-product that was dangerous to life for a short period of time. It was learned, however, that radioactivity was reduced by its action of the bioplasma. This experiment would seem to demonstrate that bioplasma is a creative force and acts opposite to nuclear force. Kozyrev states, "If mechanics enables us some day to deter and control vital processes outside organic life, operating machines will renovate (and not only exhaust) the world's potentialities. Thus, a genuine harmony between man and nature may be established. Abstract as this dream sounds, it has a realistic basis."

In analyzing these considerations, Monteith speculates that time is simply the geometrical aspect of bioplasma and is expressed as static geometry, while concentration or the focusing of energy is its dynamic aspect as expressed through dynamic geometry. The reciprocal action between static and dynamic geometry affects the processes of construction and life along with the processes of decay and death, Monteith maintains. He adds that all causes in the universe are inherent in static geometry and the effects are grounded in dynamic geometry.

"Before these ideas can be fully accepted and utilized by modern science they must be put in detailed analytical form," Monteith states. "This requires a deep understanding of the laws governing the creative processes of nature. Thus far, the necessary understanding has not been obtained by those, like myself, who are investigating its subject. It is my belief that the next revolution in science will be along these lines and that it is necessary that the energy responsible for creating the universe be incorporated into modern science before the unsolved problems which science faces today can be solved. For example, there can be no Unified Field Theory until the nature of the bioplasma has been comprehended. A complete and detailed study of the Great Pyramid, by competent scientists with bioplasma in mind, may help to throw more light upon our ignorance."

That the Great Pyramid was located at a specific place for geodetic and geographical reasons seems evident, and the location of many ancient buildings apparently was determined by an alignment with stars. Alfred Watkins, in his book *The Old Straight Track,* points out that many churches in England were established in this manner. Lyle B. Borst, professor of astronomy and physics at State University of New York, Buffalo, notes in an article in *Science* that the axes of many early Christian churches in Britain were laid out on top of ancient foundations originally determined by an alignment with stars.

However, there may have been reasons other than those of a geodetic and geographical nature for the location of the Great Pyramid and a number of other ancient structures, including pyramids in other parts of the world. In *The View Over Atlantis,* John Michell proposes that the entire surface of the earth is marked with the traces of a gigantic work of prehistoric engineering, the remains of a once universal system of natural magic, involving the use of polar magnetism together with another positive force related to solar energy. "Perhaps we all live within the ruins of an ancient structure, whose vast size has hitherto rendered it invisible," Michell states. In other words, the Great Pyramid, et al, were constructed at specific spots because of the natures of the energy force-fields at these locations. Michell discusses the work of Watkins and his studies of these ancient locations and paths, known as leys:

"It was as if some flow of current followed the course

of these manmade alignments. Members of the Straight Track Club reported instances of birds and animals migrating along certain fixed lines, described the dead straight antelope paths of the Himalayas, and wrote papers on the regular systems of tracks and landmarks in Norway, Palestine, Africa, and America. Watkins himself, an expert bee-keeper and photographer, noticed how bees, taken away and released at some distance from their hives, first describe hesitant circles in the air, and then, as if tuning in to some invisible current, make a 'bee-line' for home. While making a study of ants, he became interested in the little hills these insects throw up. His deep love of the countryside and knowledge of its ways, particularly since its hidden structure had been revealed in the discovery of leys, had given him a true understanding of the conformity of all aspects of life and growth, both large and small, to certain basic patterns. With the eye of a natural philosopher he perceived the correspondences throughout nature. Ant hills, he observed, fall into certain patterns and alignments. Like the sighting mounds upon leys, they are conical and flat topped, covered with turf.

"Evidently stone circles were originally sited according to some principle which we have yet to rediscover. By an act of divination, perhaps by the invocation of some now unrecognized force, the true sacred centres of the country became known. Remarkable confirmation of the former existence of some such system can be found in a legend which occurs all over the British Isles. According to this legend, the holy places, the sites of ancient and traditional sanctity, were first revealed in the performance of a magical rite, through some divine omen, in dreams or visions. There can be no doubt that the early Chritians looked for a sign from heaven to guide them to the spot where a church or cathedral was to be built. The fact that in almost every case the chosen site was already one of traditional sanctity indicates that their practice of divination was inherited from their predecessors. The methods used to discover the correct site for a church were the same as those by which the sites of stone circles and astronomical mounds had been located thousands of years earlier. Evidently they had much in common with the methods used by modern dowsers.

"According to all tradition the most important stage in the construction of a sacred building is the location of a suitable site, one where the spiritual forces of the locality combine to the best advantage. Whereas today it is considered in no way incongruous to determine the site of a new church by purely secular considerations, the priest of former times would as soon have built a water mill in the desert as place a church on a spot where the sacred influences were absent. The practice of divination, by which the true holy centres can be located has now lapsed so that, while our older churches are still capable of use as precise instruments for spiritual invocation, many of those built in modern times are nothing more than empty halls.

"From the numerous accounts of churches whose sites were discovered by some form of magic, it is evident that a traditional system of geomancy was practised all over the British Isles up to a few hundred years ago. Almost every cathedral and many parish churches are said to have been founded with divine guidance, revealed in dreams, through portents or by some supernatural event. These stories, which can be found in the pages of every volume of country folklore, are so numerous that only a few typical examples can be given, but these few show something of the methods by which the centres of inherent sanctity were formerly made known, and why it is that so many churches still stand directly upon prehistoric alignments.

"Behind the accumulation of brick and mortar, sited for temporary utilitarian reasons, which now smothers much of the landscape, there is still visible another layer, a network of lines and centres, arranged according to a system quite unknown today. All we have to explain the existence of this remarkable pattern is the legend that in former times there was a way of locating auspicious sites by magic. The stories themselves relate to some outward practice by which the diviner was led to the correct spot. The Druids had certain ways of achieving the ecstasy of direct communication with nature and the spirit. Like Alfred Watkins thousands of years later, they acquired a microscopic knowledge of the countryside. . . .

"A hundred years ago the practice of Chinese geomancy first became generally known in the West through the complaints of European businessmen, who found inexplicable resistance to their rational plans for exploiting the country. Continually they were informed that their railways and factories could not take certain routes or occupy certain positions. The reasons given were impossible to understand, for they had no relevance, economic, social or political, to the problem of laying out an industrial network. The Europeans were told that a certain range of hills was a terrestrial dragon and that no cutting could be made through its tail. Tunnels through dragon hills were forbidden, and a proposed railway to run straight across low, flat country was rejected on the grounds that the line would spoil the view from the hills. All this was laid down by practitioners of the science of fung-shui, 'wind and water,' obscurely explained as 'that which can not be seen and can not be grasped.'

"It has been suggested by modern Chinese nationalist writers that fung-shui was in effect a kind of town and country planning measure, an attempt at preserving the harmony of the countryside. Certainly the practice of fung-shui gave the landscape a quality of beauty and order totally beyond the achievement of any modern Western planner. This was because it was based not on merely secular considerations, but on a sublime metaphysical system in which scientific and poetic truth harmoniously united.

"Geomancers, exponents of fung-shui, were consulted

over the erection and siting of any building or tomb anywhere in China, and over the placing of any tree, post or stone which might affect the appearance and nature of the countryside. It was recognized that certain powerful currents, lines of magnetism, run invisible over the whole surface of the earth. The task of the geomancer was to detect these currents and interpret their influence on the land over which they passed."

According to Michell, there is a great scientific instrument sprawled over the globe. "At some periods, perhaps it was about 4,000 years ago, almost every corner of the world was visited by a group of men who came with a particular task to accomplish," he states. "With the help of some remarkable power, by which they could cut and raise enormous blocks of stone, these men erected vast astronomical instruments, circles of erect pillars, pyramids, underground tunnels, cyclopean stone platforms, all linked together by a network of tracks and alignments, whose course from horizon to horizon was marked by stones, mounds and earthworks. W. J. Perry in *Children of the Sun* traces the progress of these people across the Pacific, pointing out as an example of their amazing achievements the number of remote, uninhabitable islands bearing the ruins of great laborious pyramids and megalithic structures. Whether this enormous surge of energy, which within a few hundred years covered the whole earth with stone circles and earthworks, was released from one group or race, or whether it flowed spontaneously as a wave of universal inspiration is not yet clear. It appears to some that while the stone circles of northern Europe were built by the native inhabitants, those of Polynesia were the work of prehistoric missionaries. Yet Stonehenge, the latest and most perfect circle in Britian, has more in common with Crete than the native tradition, while local variations in the design and operation of astronomical structures indicates that every race made its own contribution towards a universal civilization.

"No one knows how the world-wide task was achieved, still less why. And this, of course, is the ultimate question. If we know why these people outside the range of written history devoted their entire skill and resources to the construction of a terrestrial pattern that measured both the earth and the heavens, we would know the secret of their universal civilization, a state which now seems hopelessly elusive."

Michell wonders if many of the prehistoric structures weren't constructed to measure the earth's magnetic fields. He states, "Of all the astronomical events that influence the earth's magnetic field the most dramatic is an eclipse of the sun or moon. When this takes place, the magnetic activity, normally stimulated by the eclipsed body greatly diminishes with considerable effect on the regular flow of terrestrial current. It is therefore highly significant that the ultimate purpose of many of the prehistoric stone observatories of Britian and elsewhere was the accurate prediction of lunar eclipses. An eclipse of the moon has no apparent physical influence on the earth other than in the effect it produces on the level of terrestrial magnetism."

Later in the book Michell states: "There are many stories from Hawaii and Polynesia of the foolishness of the first Christian priests who insisted on building their chuches at random instead of on their appropriate sites and thereby brought misfortune to themselves and their cause. The lines of dragon current refers to some natural flow of force, related to the earth's magnetic field and only rediscovered in modern times by the late Wilhelm Reich who called it orgone energy. . . .

"If we accept the evidence for the former existence of a universal civilization, it must be assumed that the cataclysm that engulfed it, one of those recurring events by which the shape of continents is suddenly altered, disturbed the existing pattern of magnetic current and created a new terrestrial centre. With the former capital destroyed, perhaps submerged, the survivors of the disaster would have first located this place, and would have erected a new powerful instrument as the first stage in reestablishing control over the earth's magnetic field. And here at the very centre of all the continents of the world we find the Great Pyramid."

The Great Pyramid has always been the scene of mysterious events and strange happenings. As with the Sphinx, whose early morning cry might remind one of the twang of the bow string at the close of Chekov's *Cherry Orchard,* the Great Pyramid has been said to vibrate at times with a weird sound. Tourist guides claim to reproduce this sound by striking the coffer in the King's Chamber with a stick. And local Arabs have reported at times seeing the Great Pyramid bathed in a peculiar light. A number of years ago William Groff, along with members of the Institut Egyptien, reported seeing a light or what they described as a flame rising from the Pyramid. Other reports tell of unusual circular lights near the stone structure and recently even flying objects of some nature hovering near the apex. Yet, whatever the nature of the energy fields in and around the Great Pyramid, and whatever forces of nature and the cosmos the ancient builders set out to control through its construction, these forces are still present and capable of being reinvoked when we come to recognize their function.

12. HOME EXPERIMENTS

The new awe in an ancient wonder launched by the discovery that miniature pyramids constructed on the scale of the Great Pyramid of Gizeh have within them unusual energy fields has a certain contagious quality about it. Persons from all walks of life seem to be intrigued by the promise of pyramid power. Each time we give a talk or appear on radio or television we are deluged by telephone calls and visitors. They seek more information; they want to initiate some experiments. The appeal is not difficult to understand for pyramid research to date holds out to every explorer a promise as seductive as drilling an oil well, panning for gold, or digging for ancient artifacts. The gamble is likely better, the investment considerably less, and the goal substantially more far-reaching.

What is so peculiarly attractive about pyramid research is the possibility of gain on so many different fronts. It relates to our physical bodies, our states of mind, our environment, our food, water, and air, our energy needs; it

192

touches base with nearly all aspects of life. Such an offering speaks to high adventure of heroic proportions.

This chapter is directed to those who wish to carry out some experiments on their own, with pyramids and with several other devices. For those who wish to read more on the subjects mentioned in this book, we have included a bibliography at the end of the book. However, it is in the field of experiment that the greatest adventure is to be experienced. Pyramid research or, for that matter, research of energy force-fields in general, is still in its infancy and the home experimenter can feel the thrill of exploring new territory. When the breakthroughs occur, as they surely will, he can feel a part of this pioneering effort, and it is quite possible that he can make a real contribution to the growing body of knowledge. What is needed at this stage of the game are experimenters whose greatest talents reside in the patience to keep working and watching, who have an insatiable curiosity, and are willing to exercise their creativity in finding new ways of looking at old observations. Money is not required for these experiments. Most of the materials are those to be found in the usual home workshop, or they can be purchased for a few dollars at local lumberyards and hardware stores.

The plans and schematics included in this chapter are ones we have used. Some we have designed ourselves and others have been passed along to us by experimenters whose only interest was to share what they have learned with others. We are passing them to the reader in this same spirit. This kind of sharing needs to be continued and expanded. Good communication between experimenters will go a long way in furthering the body of knowledge in this field. In this manner, we can learn from each other and avoid unnecessary duplication. We would be pleased to learn the results of any experiments in this field, as would various research groups mentioned throughout this book.

The experimenter should bear in mind that we are working in an area of sensitive energy fields. The evidence to date would indicate that these energy fields are shared by all life forms. As such, neither objects nor individuals can be considered as isolated from one another. We have learned from Backster, Vogel, Tiller, Mitchell, et al, that even such subtle forces as thoughts and emotions are constructed of energy, influenced by and influencing everything else. The extent of this "everything else" is impossible to determine at this point in time. It obviously means the immediate environment; how far extended and under what conditions is not known. What this means to the experimenter, in home workshop or large laboratory, is that he cannot divorce himself from the experiment. He is one of the unknowns to be found.

Obviously, there is no way to block or eliminate the various influences. What we can do is take into consideration those factors in the immediate vicinity of the experiment that might influence the results—electrical currents, presence of plants, animals, humans, radio and television waves, lights, metal roofing, siding or insulation inhibiting or enhancing electromagnetic fields, etc. If the experimental and control objects are subjected to the same influences, at least any differences in results between the two will be meaningful. We need to keep the variables as identical as possible.

It is more difficult to control ourselves as a component of the experiment. We can't be sure to what extent our energy fields, our emotional reactions, and thoughts will have an influence We may overtly treat the experimental object exactly the same as the control object, but our attitudes and feelings remain as uncontrolled factors. For example, we likely will want a plant within a pyramid to behave differently from one outside. Will this desire be communicated to the plant and affect its reactions? It has been demonstrated that humans unconsciously send telepathic messages. If so, these are another uncontrollable factor. This is not to discourage the experimenter. Quite the contrary, for we may learn something about ourselves. What it does mean, however, is that we use double-blind approaches when we can. This would be difficult with plants placed inside pyramids. It will work on such experiments as treatment of water which is then used for watering plants. We can mark the containers, mix them up, and not know which is which until the end of the experiment. We can use plates or foil treated inside pyramids and then used as psychotronic generators in the above manner by marking them and hiding this information from ourselves. Treated razor blades can be marked by ourselves, then shuffled so that we do not know which is which, and then given to a second party for testing, who also does not know which blade he is using.

It is also a great help in confirming our results if we can enlist the interest of associates or friends and have them duplicate our experiments. We then have a way of checking our results. The more people involved in the experiments, the better. Also by way of validating efforts, recruit family members, friends, and neighbors to witness as many phases of your projects as possible.

It is wise to mark experimental and control objects clearly so there is no question as to their identity. It is also useful to keep a regular log on experiments, jotting down dates, measurements, results, etc., daily or on whatever schedule that is appropriate. Make your measurements as accurate as possible and where appropriate carefully weigh materials or objects, such as food items and liquids. Take careful notice of any differences in moisture, air currents, light, etc., affecting experimental and control objects.

The above considerations apply to research projects in general. We can now direct our attention to the construction and use of various devices.

Pyramids can be made from most any kind of material as research to date points to the effectiveness resulting from the shape rather than to the material used in its construction. Metal, however, does appear to block some of the electro-magnetic forces (although not all forces), but wood, plastics, canvas, and fiberglass all seem to work equally well. Although it probably is unnecessary, if you want to be a real purist, you can avoid any metal in your pyramid by using wooden dowels and glue instead of nails.

Pyramids can be any size, from one inch tall to building size. At this writing, the Unity Church of Christianity in Houston, Texas, has under construction a church built on the exact scale of the Great Pyramid. The idea originated with the church's minister, John D. Rankin, but has reportedly caught the imagination of the entire congregation. The church will have an 89-foot square base, will stand over 63 feet tall, and cover an area of 9,206 square feet. A staff member of the Burde Baker Planetarium in Houston helped align the building on the north-south axis. A friend of ours in Mexico has informed us that he plans to build a warehouse in the shape of a pyramid for storage of eggs, and we have been told that there are plans for building a large pyramid-shaped restaurant in Denver.

The size of the pyramid is largely determined by its intended use. Razor blades have been effectively sharpened in four-inch pyramids. However, if the plan is to place an object at a particular level of the pyramid, such as the King's Chamber, the pyramid has to be large enough to accommodate it at that level. If the object takes up too much of the inner space, the experiment will be less effective. For example, a pyramid should be about 18 inches tall for experiments with plant seedlings. A pyramid large enough to accommodate a gallon of water should be three to four feet tall. The pyramids we have used for meditation, where the person is sitting or lying down, have been six feet tall.

A base is not required for the pyramid. It is sometimes difficult, however, to stabilize the pyramid and keep it squared without a base, particularly when it is made of lightweight material. If you find a base necessary, it is preferable to anchor it permanently to the pyramid. This will necessitate an opening or door through which to place objects. This can be accomplished by using one side as the opening. Tape one edge securely and fasten the other edge with just enough tape to hold it in place. With large pyramids, you can either make one side so it will open on hinges or construct a door. If the pyramid is to be made of rigid materials such as boards or plywood, you can simply cut the door in one side and hinge this same piece. If the pyramid is to be made of wood frame and covered with plastic, it will be necessary to run a frame board from one side to the other at the height of the door, and two frame boards on each side of the door from the top frame board to the base. You will then want to build a rectangular frame the size of the door opening and cover it with plastic.

There are several ways to determine the correct dimensions for the pyramid. One way is to figure that for every one foot of height you will need 1.5708 feet of base and 1.4945 feet of side, that is from the corner to the apex. For example, if you wanted a pyramid six feet tall, then each side of your square base would be 9.4248 feet and each upright triangular side would be 8.9674 feet.

You might find the following scale useful in constructing smaller pyramids:

	Height		Base	Side	
7.5a =	3"	(11.91)	4.71"	4.48"	10.33 cm
10 cm	4"	15.89	6.28"	5.98"	14.62 cm
12.5 cm	5"	19.86	7.85"	7.47"	18.92 cm
15 cm	6"	23.89	9.42"	8.98"	22.91 cm
20 cm	8"	31.77	12.57"	11.96"	30.89 cm
one 2 feet	10"	39.2	15.70"	14.95"	38.87 cm
30 cm	12"	47.26	18.85"	17.93"	46.86 cm
six feet			9.4248 feet	8.674 feet	
182 cm			287.2679 cm	273.3263 cm	

Another way to figure the dimensions is to take the length of the base and subtract five percent for the sides, although this method is not quite as accurate as the above scale. Still a third method is to take a protractor and draw the sides at 61 degrees to the base. This method can be used for any size pyramid and eliminates the need for figuring the dimensions.

When the sides of the pyramid are in place they will form an angle to the base of 51 degrees and 51 minutes, a miniature replica of the Great Pyramid.

It is best to place the pyramid in a room away from radios, television sets, and other electrical appliances. Actually it would be even better to locate the pyramid outside or in a room away from any metal sheeting or electrical wiring, but this may be difficult to do. The pyramid should be placed on the floor or on a stable pedestal or table to keep it from being bumped and knocked out of alignment.

The pyramid must be aligned on the four cardinal points—north, east, south, and west. This means that each of the four sides face one of the cardinal points. You can draw a straight line through the center of the pyramid or simply use one of the sides as your north-south axis. A compass can be used to align the pyramid on magnetic north. True north would be more accurate, but according to all reports magnetic north appears to work as well. True north varies from magnetic north by several degrees of declination, depending on the latitude where you live. The declination for your area can be learned by consulting a local almanac or calling a local airport.

Much of the research to date has focused on the area of the King's Chamber. In placing research objects in this location, measure a distance vertically one-third of the distance from the base to the apex and directly below the apex. Objects can be placed on nonconductive boxes, blocks, or pedestals at this level. However, the pedestal should be no larger than necessary.

When placing an item in the pyramid, orient it so that the longest portion is in the direction of the north-south axis. When running tests with experimental and control objects, you may wish to place the control specimen under a box with the same volume as the pyramid. In the case of plants, ventilation should be provided for either at the bottom of the pyramid and control box or in the sides.

When sharpening razor blades, after a blade has been used several times place it at the one-third level in the pyramid, edges facing east and west, and leave it there for at least a week. The blade can then be used for shaving and replaced immediately afterward in the pyramid. Dull blades, knives, and scissors can be sharpened in the pyramid but must remain there unmoved for a period of four months.

If you wish to test your pyramid for the amount of energy being emanated through the apex, use either a pendulum or a dowsing rod. A pendulum can be made with any small heavy object, such as a roller bearing or metal nut attached to a string. Slowly move toward the pyramid while suspending the pendulum from your hand and slightly above the apex. The pendulum will likely move when you get within a half foot of the apex of the pyramid. Try suspending the pendulum directly above the apex and you will probably find that the pendulum weight moves slightly away in one direction or another or it may make a slow circle around the apex.

Dowsing rods can be made from two metal rods around three feet long. Coat hangers can be used by straightening them out. Turn down about seven inches of each rod at 90-degree angles for the handles. Grasp the rods so that they are parallel to each other and pointing away from you. Move toward the pyramid so that the rods will bracket the pyramid above the level of the apex. As the tips of the rods approach the apex, the rods will cross each other or swing away from each other. You will find that the energy field radiating from the apex is cone shaped and has a widening diameter as it rises.

We have found when using a pyramid for meditation that sitting on a pillow and facing north seems to work better than facing other directions. When lying down, we use a cot and lie with our head to the north. In recent tests conducted by Gary Piapp of Huma-Tech Industries, manufacturers of biofeedback equipment, George Cooper, president of Pyrameditation, Inc., and Bill Cox, editor of *Pyramid Guide,* the brainwave activity of subjects meditating inside a pyramid showed marked increase in amplitude regularity, and alpha and theta brainwave production. A comparison was made with the same meditating subjects first tested outside the pyramid a few minutes prior to entering the pyramid.

A number of people have asked us about constructing houses in the pyramid shape. We have cautioned them on using aluminum siding or aluminum-faced insulation due to its apparent blocking or absorbing quality of electromagnetic forces. It well may be, as mentioned in the chapter, "Effects On Solids," that once the aluminum has become saturated with pyramid energy it no longer serves as a barrier to the force and can even be used as a psychotronic generator. It should be remembered, however, that while aluminum foil will absorb the energy it also loses it within a few days. Also, the aluminum was treated inside the pyramid. Aluminum siding would be on the outside of the pyramid and our tests, though far from exhaustive, show no indication that aluminum can be effectively treated on the outside of the pyramid. Until more research is done on this matter our suggestions would be for an individual thinking of using aluminum siding on a pyramid-shaped building to first construct an exact prototype of the structure and run a series of tests over a period of time.

The pyramid shape does not readily lend itself to space economy but on the sides where the walls meet the deck storage space could be provided. We believe the doors should be positioned so that when closed no hindrance to the interior pyramid shape will result. In other words, we believe that the dormer-type windows should not be used unless glass is installed to conform to the slope of the walls, where the dormer meets the edge of the roof slope. Probably electrical wiring should be placed near the base, with leads running upward to wall outlets. This will eliminate electric currents circling the pyramid shape.

We have noticed and others have commented on the freshness of the air in our shop where there are a number of pyramids. There also seems to be an absence of odor. It might be that a series of pyramids placed in the attic of a house might work as purifiers if aligned on the north-south axis. The pyramids might reduce stale air odors, and alleviate tobacco and cooking odors.

The artists' renditions in the photo section show some of the dazzling possibilities of pyramid house construction.

13. THE PYRAMID: WINDOW TO THE UNIVERSE

"So above, so below; so below, so above" is a philosophical adage of some vintage, but it has been gaining in
scientific favor the more we probe the infinity of space
and the finiteness of subnuclear particles. The atomic
structure of the universe seems to repeat itself whether we
view the solar system or ponder electrons spinning about
their nucleus. And now our solar system in the immense
stretch of space inhabited by immeasurable galaxies is so
overwhelmed by comparison that it appears but a whirling electron itself. Yet, peering into an electron microscope, one could just as easily imagine the display as
something seen through the most powerful of telescopes.
The pattern remains the same; only the point of reference
has changed.

One might justifiably theorize that somewhere below
our level of measuring subnuclear particles some inhabi-
tant views one of these particles as his planet, or that
somewhere out in space some intelligence announces that

it has just discovered a more minute atomic unit little knowing that he refers to our earth. It really doesn't seem to matter in which direction we travel, we soon pass beyond the threshold of our perceptions and infinity overcomes us. We have now learned that space and time have only the limited reality of points of reference. Solids have long disappeared, replaced by vortices of energy and energy, in turn, quickly loses its identity in consciousness.

Having lost the trail, we start over, making chalk marks on thought-forms hoping to find our way home again. Of all the rocks we have peered beneath and written laws unto, one has escaped our scrutiny and refused to pamper us with the delusion of truth. Knowledge of the Pyramid has been particularly frustrating because it is man-made. It is one thing for God to have secrets, but to be unable to decipher an artifact of a fellow creature is more than a little embarrassing. It is a sobering experience to brilliant minds.

One finds it difficult not to speak in mysterious tones when referring to the Great Pyramid for something rather peculiar has been going on there for as long as man can remember. Everything about it is shrouded in mystery: its age, designers, builders, construction, purpose. Other things we have taken apart—molecules, protoplasms, radio waves—toyed with, and duplicated. The Great Pyramid has not allowed this. Everytime that we have paused on the edge of an answer, it eludes us. A variable changes, a second glance reveals a different picture, data is missing, or new information suddenly comes to light. It happened three years ago with efforts to measure cosmic ray penetration, and everything went well enough until a replay of the tapes revealed that the patterns were not the same from day to day. It happened again as late as December 1974, when the Stanford Research Institute-Ain Shams University expedition abruptly halted operations. The American and Egyptian scientists used short-range radio waves in hopes of seeing through the pyramid's sides and spot hidden chambers. The mission was abandoned before it reached the halfway point after the radar signals, transmitted by a 30,000-volt sounder, disappeared after traveling only a few feet because of the pyramid's unexpectedly high moisture content. The latest report was that physicists have gone back to the drawing board. What will it be next time? Unusual crystal formations serving as blocking mechanisms? Erratic electromagnetic currents altering instrument readouts?

Those of us with our wooden and plastic pyramid miniatures have come up with some extremely interesting data, but we, too, have been confronted with mysteries, with the unexpected, with turnabouts, and these exceptions to the rule neatly put down theories: a plant suddenly alters its behavior; metal reverses its polarity; a razor blade still stays sharp but has days of dullness or acts differently than a companion blade; sound comes and goes; one sample of milk turns to yogurt and a second simply dehydrates; a compass held over the pyramid's apex swings to and fro one day and lies dormant the next. While we can always truthfully say in reference to our pyramids that something is going on in there that is not happening on the outside, we cannot always be sure what that something is. Working with models has a distinct advantage, however. We can re-tool, reassess, make adjustments, and run tests with many pyramids.

Somewhere in the long history of pyramid exploration there is a punch line, a moral to the story. Let's assume for the moment that the builders of the Great Pyramid knew exactly what they were doing, that they were in possession of some valuable knowledge and that they incorporated this information within the Pyramid. If so, why would they take such great pains to keep the knowledge hidden? Can we assume that they would do so for the same reason that anyone imparts or withholds information—that the would-be recipient would understand or would fail to understand and possibly use the information unwisely? The great religious teachers have always presented their messages on both the exoteric and esoteric levels. Those who had ears could hear and those who had eyes could see, meaning the possession of insights greater than some of their peers. In fact, so multi-level were the teachings that their truths would unfold as the student developed greater and greater insights. The teachings could sustain him at whatever intellectual and spiritual level he happened to be. This, at least, was the practice of the ancient Mystery Schools, and the early inhabitants of Egypt were the pioneers in this field. If this was their style for portioning out knowledge at a safe rate, it seems reasonable to assume that they would not alter this plan as regards the Pyramid. Somehow they must have known that it would take centuries before man would be ready to handle the knowledge contained in the Great Pyramid, so they built it to last for centuries, to remain undaunted by earthquakes and the winds of time, invulnerable to chisel and hammer, to radar and physics, stoically awaiting until man himself became the tool that could open its doors. "Open Sesame" still depends on hidden knowledge. What better sentry before the portals of wisdom than the enigmatical Sphinx—strange hybrid of beast and man and god—smiling faintly perhaps at man's bewilderment to gain entrances sealed only by himself.

The truths have been scattered along the passageways and tunnels of the Great Pyramid. This Mount Olympus has offered up its secrets not begrudgingly but in a fashion that men had to work for them and in so doing had to grow, had to reach, had to sharpen more his perceptors than his chisels. If the task had been easy, what follies would men have committed in his infancy and adolescence? Would the knowledge have been ignored, trampled in the dust and forgotten, abused? In what century of recorded history would the information contained therein have been used wisely? Is this now the century, the season, the hour, for its unveiling? Certainly, we stand in desperate need of a greater knowledge—of feeding a world, of new energy sources, of inner awareness and control. Is need alone the key? Not likely, it would seem, unless accompanied by understanding. Perhaps the current interest in pyramids is witness to a widespread effort to learn more. Pyramidia is no longer limited to a handful of scientists storming a stone mountain. Awareness of "pyramid power" has brought expeditions into the basement laboratory, and those who can not journey to Gizeh are paraphrasing the Islamic tenet that if Mohammed can't go to the hill, then the hill must come to Mohammed.

Strangely enough, if information gleaned from the pyramid had been complete in itself, man would have surmised that he had uncovered the secret and that would have likely been the extent of the search. But pieces of information were uncovered, occasionally startling, more than likely controversial, but at no juncture complete. Always the material either depended upon additional data or hinted at other knowledge. Man has never been able to say, "Well, we know all there is to know about the pyramid and now we can go on to other things." Fragments of truth have served as a carrot on a string.

Some of these fragments have indicated that the pyramid is a microcosm of the universe: its schematics unfold a map of the world and the heavens; its shape represents the geometrical constructs of nature; its interior and exterior measurements depict the mathematical relationships of universal truths; its construction incorporates archetypal symbols; and its purpose has been to not only provide an indestructable encyclopedia of man and his world but a receptical or generator of cosmic energy. It has been proposed that the energy within the pyramid incorporates the entire spectrum of energy fields, known and unknown. This energy is viewed as the total energy complex, referred to in ancient literature as Prana or Chi, and in contemporary studies as biocosmic and psychotronic.

Mystics are now saying that science is beginning to confirm their conceptions of a singular energy field, and the oneness of all things.

Certainly, at least, the energy force-field within pyramid space appears singular and yet manifold as to its involvement in and effect upon a range of substances or states from dense crystallizations to nonmaterial consciousness. The bridging from the material to the immaterial by a medium that apparently is both does not present a dilemma to those scientists who consider mind and matter as the extremities of a singular substance. Such a concept is not contradictory in the Indian cosmological system in which it really matters very little whether we view existence as being material with spirit being its more rarified form or whether we consider existence as spiritual with matter being its most densified form.

In the Tibetan Buddhist model of substance, mineral is primarily dense physical with a slight expansion of etheric physical; plants are dense physical, etheric physical, with a slight expansion of emotional substance; animals are dense physical, etheric physical, emotional, and with a slight expansion of mental substance; and man incorporates all of these and has a slight expansion of spiritual matter. Thus all life is linked together in an evolutionary movement toward pure spirit. Certainly, satisfactory explanations for mind over matter are hard to come by when we persist in a separation of the nature of each, and are much easier with which to cope when we consider all life forms, including thought-forms, as fields and vortices of energy existing somewhere along a single continuum. The whole field of psychic phenomena appears more viable within such a scheme. And the increasing amount of evidence that pyramid power can effect changes of both a material and immaterial nature appears more substantial within this cosmological model.

In the final analysis, perhaps, energy escapes into consciousness and the world becomes a thought. And therein may reside a clue to the sometimes erratic behavior of pyramid power. We can control all the variables—light, heat, air, moisture, etc.—but there is one variable of which we know little and over which we have gained only superficial control: ourselves. This it would appear is one unstable component of our experiments. Former astronaut Edgar Mitchell told us this when he said that we are reaching the outer limits of our ability to probe the unknown. In order to go further in our observations, he said, we would need to examine the observer; no longer can the experimenter be isolated from the experiment. Man is integrally involved in everything that he examines, Mitchell stated.

As with all other research, then, with our pyramid investigations we are faced with the ultimate unknown— man himself. If all roads lead to consciousness, in the end we must understand it or the journey is ended before the goal is won.

Is this the mandate from the Great Pyramid? Is its greatest service as a mirror to reflect ourselves? If so, it would agree with the counsel of the Delphic Oracle "Man, know thyself." If this message carries the highest priority of the ancients, might not this be their proudest monument?

What is the future role of the Great Pyramid and its progeny? Will the structure itself reveal chambers of knowledge? Will our research provide answers to new energy sources? Will the pyramid shape elevate our consciousness in order that new knowledge can be gained? Perhaps all three questions can be answered in the affirmative, but the path seems clear: We must find—as Paul Brunton's white-robed host explained—the pyramid *within* in order to comprehend the pyramid without.

The venture appears not only worthwhile but even mandatory. The gravest problems facing mankind today, we are told, are food shortages, pollution, a depletion of energy sources, and war. And the pyramid offers some promise of meeting these needs: 1) Food shortages—through seed germination, increased plant growth, and food preservation; 2) pollution—early tests reveal that pyramid space can purify water, air, and soil; 3) energy sources—through generation or enhancement of known and unknown energy fields; 4) war—the alternative, of course, is peace and world thinkers would lead us to believe that peace is dependent upon man's greater understanding and elevation of consciousness. The pyramid shows promise of serving as an initiator of higher levels of awareness.

Life, indeed, does move in mysterious circles, and experience has a way of remembering itself. It may be that the historians have been right all along, that knowing the past is imperative to understanding the present and projecting the future. Perhaps the pyramid is a window to both the past and the future.

BIBLIOGRAPHY

Airola, P.O. *Health Secrets from Europe.* West Nyack, N.Y.: Parker Publishing Co., 1970.

Backster, C. "Evidence of a Primary Perception in Plant Life," *International Journal of Parapsychology,* 10:4, 1968.

Beck, B. "The Russian Lakhovsky Rejuvenation Machine," Borderland Sciences Research Foundation.

Bell, A.M. *Practical Dowsing—A Symposium.* London: G. Bell & Sons, 1965.

Benavides, R. *Dramatic Prophesies of the Great Pyramid.* Mexico City: Editores Mexicanos Unidos, 1970.

Blavatsky, M.P. *The Secret Doctrine.* Los Angeles: Theosophical Society, 1930.

Bolton, B. *The Secret Power of Plants.* New York: Berkley Medallion Books, 1974.

Bose, J.C.B. *Plant Response.* London: Longrams, Green & Co., 1906.

Brown, J. "I Discover the Immortal B-Cell," Borderland Sciences Research Foundation publications.

Brunes, T. *The Secrets of Ancient Geometry*. Copenhagen: Chrones, 1967.

Brunton, P. *A Search in Sacred Egypt*. London: Rider, 1936.

_____. *The Wisdom of the Overself*. New York: E. P. Dutton & Co., 1943.

Castaneda, C. *The Teachings of Don Juan*. Berkeley: University of California Press, 1968.

Charroux, R. *One Hundred Thousand Years of Man's Unknown History*. New York: Berkley, 1970.

Clement, M. *The Waves that Heal*. Sussex, England: Health Science Press, 1949.

Cox, W. E. "The Effect of PK on Electrochemical Systems," *Journal of Parapsychology*, 29:165, 1965.

Davidson, D. *The Great Pyramid: Its Divine Message*. London: Williams and Norgate, 1924.

Eden, Jerome. *Orgone Energy*. Copyright © Exposition Press. Excerpts appear on pages 51-53.

Edwards, I.E.S. *The Pyramids of Egypt*. Middlesex, England: Penguin, 1949.

Eeman, L.E. *The Curative Properties of Human Radiations*. London: Frederick Muller Ltd., 1947.

Eisenbud, J. *The World of Ted Serios*. London: Jonathan Cape, 1968.

Evans-Wentz, J.D. *The Tibetan Book of the Dead*. Oxford: University Press, 1949.

Flanagan, G.P. "The Pyramid and Its Relationship to Biocosmic Energy," Glendale, Calif.: Flanagan, 1972.

Frei, E. H. "Medical Application of Magnetism," *Bulletin of the Atomic Scientists*, October 1972.

Garrett, E. *Adventures in the Supernormal*. New York: Garrett Publishers, 1959.

_____. *Many Voices*. New York: G. P. Putnam's Sons, 1968.

Geddes, P. *The Life and Work of Sir Jagadis C. Bose.* London: Geddes, Longmans, Green & Co., 1920.

Gauquelin, M. *The Cosmic Clocks.* London: Peter Owen, 1969.

Ghadiali, D.P. *Spectro-Chrome Metry Encyclopedia.* Malaga, N.J.: Spectro-Chrome Institute, 1939.

Grad, B. "A Telekinetic Effect on Plant Growth," *International Journal of Parapsychology,* 6:473, 1964.

Hall, M.P. *The Secret Teachings of All Ages.* Los Angeles: Philosophical Research Society, 1969.

Hicks, C.B. "Growing Corn to Music," *Popular Mechanics,* May 1963.

Hills, C. *Nuclear Evolution.* London: Centre Community Publications, 1968.

Jeans, J. *The Mysterious Universe.* New York: Dover Publications, 1968.

Kervran, L. *Biological Transmutations.* Binghamton, N.Y.: Swan House, 1972.

Keyes, L.E. *Toning—The Creative Power of the Voice.* Santa Monica, Calif.: DeVorss & Co., 1973.

Kirlian, S.D. and Kirlian, V. "Photography and Visual Observations by Means of High-Frequency Currents," translation by Foreign Technology Division, United States Air Force Systems Command, 1963.

Krippner, S. and Rubin, D., eds. *The Human Aura in Acupuncture and Kirlian Photography.*

Layne, N.M. and Crabb, R.H. "Vitic or Magnetic Vitality," Borderland Sciences Research Foundation publication.

Lehner, M. "Egypt—Reflections on a Tour," *A.R.E. Journal.*

Lissmann, H.W. "Electric Location by Fishes," *Scientific American,* March 1963.

Loehr, F. *The Power of Prayer on Plants.* New York: New American Library, 1969.

Michell, J. *The View Over Atlantis.* New York: Ballantine Books, 1969.

Mitchell, E.D. *Psychic Exploration.* New York: G. P. Putnam's Sons, 1974.

Monroe, R. A. *Journeys Out of the Body.* New York: Doubleday, 1973.

Moss, T. and Johnson, K. "Radiation Field Photography," *Psychic* magazine, July 1972.

Ostrander, S. and Schroeder, L. *Psychic Discoveries Behind the Iron Curtain.* Englewood Cliffs, N.J.: Prentice-Hall, 1971.

Pierrakos, J. C. "The Energy Field in Man and Nature," Institute of Bioenergetic Analysis, New York.

Proctor, R. H. *The Great Pyramid: Observatory, Tomb, and Temple.* London: Chatto & Wendus, 1883.

Reich, W. *The Cancer Biopathy,* New York: Noonday Books, 1973.

————. *Ether, God and Devil/Cosmic Superimposition.* New York: Noonday Books, 1972.

Rhine, L. E. *Mind Over Matter.* London: Macmillan, 1970.

Roberts, J. *Seth Speaks.* Englewood Cliffs, N.J.: Prentice-Hall, 1972.

Seiss, J. A. *The Great Pyramid: A Miracle in Stone.* New York: Rudolf Steiner Publications, 1973.

Skinner, J. R. *Actual Measures of the Great Pyramid.* Toledo, Ohio: Blode, 1880.

Smyth, C. P. *New Measures of the Great Pyramid.* London: R. Banks, 1884.

Stromberg, G. "Spiritual Healing and Modern Science," in *Spiritual Healing.* Los Angeles: Science of Mind Publications, 1973.

Thomson, D. "Force Field Detectors," *Maclean's* magazine, September 1968.

Tiller, W. A. "Radionics, Radiesthesia and Physics," Unpublished manuscript.

Tompkins, Peter. *Secrets of the Great Pyramid.* New York: Harper and Row, 1971.

Tompkins, P. and Bird, C. *Secret Life of Plants*. Avon Publishing Co., 1973.

Toth, M. and Nielsen, G. *Pyramid Power*. New York: Freeway Press, 1974.

Van Tassel, G. W. Proceedings of College of Universal Wisdom, 9:11, 1972.

Von Däniken, E. *Chariots of the Gods*. London: Souvenir Books, 1969.

Walewski, S. C. *A System of Caucasian Yoga*. New York: Falcon Wing Press, 1955.

Watkins, A. *The Old Straight Track*. London: Methuen, 1925.

Watson, L. *Super Nature*. New York: Doubleday, 1973.

Weber, J. "The Detection of Gravitational Waves," *Scientific American*, 224:22, 1971.

Yogananda, P. *Autobiography of a Yoga*. Los Angeles: Self-Realization Fellowship, 1959.

INDEX

SCIENCE FACT FROM CORONET

ISAAC ASIMOV
☐ 19879 6 The Tragedy of the Moon   60p
☐ 20015 4 Asimov on Astronomy   80p
☐ 19999 7 Today and Tomorrow   60p
☐ 19984 9 Please Explain   85p

ADRIAN BERRY
☐ 19924 5 The Next Ten Thousand Years   £1.00

CARL SAGAN
☐ 19682 3 The Cosmic Connection   85p

LYALL WATSON
☐ 18833 2 Supernature   £1.00
☐ 19989 X The Romeo Error   80p
☐ 21974 2 Gifts Of Unknown Things   85p

All these books are available at your local bookshop or newsagent, or can be ordered direct from the publisher. Just tick the titles you want and fill in the form below.
Prices and availability subject to change without notice.

~~~~~~

CORONET BOOKS, P.O. Box 11, Falmouth, Cornwall.
Please send cheque or postal order, and allow the following for postage and packing:

U.K. – One book 22p plus 10p per copy for each additional book ordered, up to a maximum of 82p.

B.F.P.O. and EIRE – 22p for the first book plus 10p per copy for the next 6 Books, thereafter 4p per book.

OTHER OVERSEAS CUSTOMERS – 30p for the first book and 10p per copy for each additional book.

Name ....

Address ....

....